# Toward a Pastoral Theology of Holy Saturday

# Toward a Pastoral Theology of Holy Saturday

Providing Spiritual Care for War Wounded Souls

Adam D. Tietje

*Foreword by Deborah van Deusen Hunsinger*

WIPF & STOCK · Eugene, Oregon

TOWARD A PASTORAL THEOLOGY OF HOLY SATURDAY
Providing Spiritual Care for War Wounded Souls

Copyright © 2018 Adam D. Tietje. All rights reserved. Except for brief quotations in critical publications or reviews, no part of this book may be reproduced in any manner without prior written permission from the publisher. Write: Permissions, Wipf and Stock Publishers, 199 W. 8th Ave., Suite 3, Eugene, OR 97401.

Wipf & Stock
An Imprint of Wipf and Stock Publishers
199 W. 8th Ave., Suite 3
Eugene, OR 97401

www.wipfandstock.com

PAPERBACK ISBN: 978-1-5326-5777-1
HARDCOVER ISBN: 978-1-5326-5778-8
EBOOK ISBN: 978-1-5326-5779-5

Manufactured in the U.S.A.                    10/24/18

Unless otherwise noted, Scripture quotations are taken from the New Revised Standard Version Bible, copyright 1989, Division of Christian Education of the National Council of Churches in the United States of America. Used by permission. All rights reserved.

For Meegan, Julian, and Juno

# Contents

*Foreword by Deborah van Deusen Hunsinger* | ix

*Preface* | xiii

1. War Is Hell. Coming Home Is Hell, Too. | 1

2. The Story of Holy Saturday | 20

3. A Chalcedonian Conception of Trauma and Moral Injury | 49

4. Coming Home from the Far Country | 73

5. Ministering Between Cross and Resurrection | 96

*Bibliography* | 111

# Foreword

ANYONE WHO HAS EVER tried to imagine the traumatic suffering of those sent to fight in a war—as well as those whose lives have been indelibly shaped by such suffering—will encounter in this book a riveting account of the psychological and spiritual consequences of war on combat soldiers and veterans.

I am one who has spent much of my life in the former category (as one trying to imagine such suffering) and the author of this book is in the latter (as one who served as a military chaplain in the wars in Afghanistan). The story that unfolds—and the theological reflection on it—is compelling in part because of the author's personal witness. Not only was he wounded in battle himself but he has also listened to the inconsolable grief and agonizing guilt of soldiers whose suffering did not end the day that they returned home. The hell encountered in battle was seemingly never-ending, only to be followed by the hell of returning home. Adam Tietje has had to struggle existentially with every single issue raised in this book. Even so, the book is not an autobiographical rendition of his own story. Though it is, from time to time, appropriately alluded to, it never takes center stage. Instead, Jesus Christ and the saving power of the gospel is the central character of his narrative.

War is traumatic not only for the soldiers but also for all of us. My grandmother turned 19 in 1914, my mother in 1939. I turned 19 in 1968 and my daughter in 2002. As young women on the threshold of adulthood, all of us faced a country at war. Images from the Vietnam War still sear my mind and shatter my heart more than fifty years later. We who send soldiers to fight seem to do so with little forethought of the crippling lifelong consequences or the intergenerational trauma that will visit the children and grandchildren of these warriors. Chaplains, pastors, social workers, psychotherapists, and families intimately know the high human cost to those who survive. They see and hear the nightmares, the drug and alcohol addiction, the rampant homelessness, the depression, the mental and spiritual anguish, and the emotional and physical pain of many who return home from war. But most of us close our eyes and ears and turn away from this suffering, not wanting to see or hear about it. This book is written for those with enough courage to keep their eyes and ears open, especially for the caregivers who give of themselves to those who suffer: by listening to their stories, by praying with and for them, and by holding onto the promises of the gospel when the soldiers themselves cannot see their way out of hell.

The work is beautifully written—both methodologically sophisticated and pastorally nuanced. Adam Tietje has that rare gift of theological clarity, enabling him to distinguish between mental distress and spiritual wounds, claiming that both are suffered by those who suffer the trauma of war. He outlines how chaplains, pastors, and ordinary Christians can offer spiritual sanctuary to those who are stuck in the "far country," away from the love of God, their Father. Using the story of the "prodigal son" as his central biblical trope and drawing on the scholarship of both Karl Barth and Hans Urs von Balthasar, Tietje upholds the ancient Trinitarian claims that God's love is fully revealed, even while it is hidden, in the suffering of the Father and the Son (see Psalms 22 and 88).

Pastoral caregivers are enjoined to make Holy Saturday their own dwelling place. Even there, in the depths of Sheol, they trust God's presence. As those who trust in God, even when they cannot see how he is at work, they offer hospitality to those who return from war, wounded to the very core of their being. By trusting in the power of the resurrection of Jesus Christ, pastoral caregivers offer veterans opportunities to share their stories, give voice to their anguish and grief, confess their sins, and, by the grace and power of God, to find healing, reconciliation, and peace with the

## Foreword

God who calls them to live life anew—a life of gratitude, worship, and service.

> Deborah van Deusen Hunsinger
> Charlotte W. Newcombe Professor of Pastoral Theology
> Princeton Theological Seminary
> Princeton, New Jersey

# Preface

THE NAVY EMBLEM IN my grandfather's workshop was one of very few mementos of his military service. As a young boy, I learned that he had served during World War II. Yet, nothing he shared ever gave me any indication that he had seen battle. His role as the "oil king" aboard a troop transport ship seemed so far removed from actual combat. I imagined empty oceans and warm South Pacific winds. I must confess, part of my attraction to the army as an adolescent was that America's global dominance in the air and on the sea (this is after the collapse of the Soviet Union, mind you) made ground combat the last real arena of war. That my grandfather had no naval war stories to tell only confirmed my suspicion. I guess you could say, I was disappointed. Not that I could articulate it precisely this way at the time, but I had a sense that war revealed some truth about life and death that only those who had experienced it would be privy to know. Beyond death and destruction, it seemed to me, war was something that forged men of character and consequence. I was disappointed because my grandfather seemed so far removed from history, from consequence—in short, from war.

It was not until I returned from Afghanistan that I came to know what my grandfather meant when he said he had been to Okinawa. It always seemed like the last port of call on his Pacific cruise. I know he mentioned it, but it was always so matter of fact, like the way he casually talked about the "Japs." Even after I learned about the battle of Okinawa in history class, I always imagined my grandfather just showing up after the battle had ended. Yet, as we sat behind my grandparents house in the early July Florida heat, he talked as if he were still there. He was eighty-five when I returned from Afghanistan, but as he told me how he watched the Kamikaze pilot veer away from his ship to hit a sister vessel, he was still an eighteen year old boy. Grief overpowered him. He was still helpless in the face of such unbearable evil and horrific trauma. The bodies of young men littered the water. For his part, he helped sail a ship that sent Marines to their death on nearby beaches and he carried the guilt of survival his whole life. His troop transport ship had been christened the USS Fond du Lac, the "bottom of the lake." I suppose that is what passes for gallows humor in the Navy. His ship never did go down. He survived and returned home to finish high school, to marry my grandmother, to work, and to raise my father, his brother, and his sister.

My grandfather witnessed one of the bloodiest battles in the history of humanity and I never knew. My father never even knew. Yet, he carried the weight of these stories and images for a lifetime. Coming home from my own encounters with death, I wondered what I might be sharing with my grandson when I am eighty-five. Would my memories be as present to me as they were to him? If they are, I suppose that is my small measure of the cost of war. More importantly, in coming to know my grandfather more fully, I found the shred of hope I had been grasping for in the despair of my return. He had survived, come home, and found a way to make a life. Even as I watched so many lives unravel and some needlessly end, this is what I wanted for my soldiers and, I suppose, for me too: a way to live after war.

I do not think many of the stories that take us to war survive for the return trip. I am not sure what led my grandfather to volunteer for war—a sense of duty, a desire to escape from a cruel father, a need for a clear rite of passage to manhood, a way to control the outcome of an inevitable draft, or maybe all of that and more. I am sure that he came home with a new self-understanding, different desires, and a different relationship to war and his country (afterwards a fervent isolationist). Above all, the story he came home with was that the Christian faith and prayers of his mother carried him through. God carried him through. My grandfather found a way to give thanks for that his whole life long, even as he continued to bear the pain of survival to the very end.

I am filled with shame at my naiveté and hubris, about war, yes, and also in how I regarded my grandfather. Not only had I misjudged him on the basis of my own scale of value—he was, in fact, at the center of a very consequential history and a man whose character was shaped deeply by his time in the South Pacific—but I had been measuring with a flawed scale. War is not where boys go to become men or a forge for greatness and character. War is killing and death. Because it is so, war is everywhere and always marked by fear and anger, guilt and shame, and sorrow and sadness. But even in the shadow of death, there is love and friendship. God is good. My grandfather found this to be true and now, I, too, can attest.

I am writing this as I near the end of my time as an active duty army chaplain and prepare to return to the academy. Over the last nine years, I spent thousands of hours talking with soldiers before, during, and after war. This work comes directly out of my experiences with them and my quest for theological clarity as I sought to care for them. As the title suggests, this is a work of pastoral theology: a book for pastors, chaplains, and others who offer spiritual care to those who come home from war. While the social sciences, especially psychology, often have pride of place within pastoral theological conversations, my hope here is that I have remained firmly grounded in dogmatic theology, even as I listen to the wisdom of other teachers. Because of my interest in dogmatic (or systematic or constructive) theology, perhaps the chapters on Holy Saturday and Barth's Chalcedonian approach will hold a broader appeal. While I stand by what I have written here, I have more recently come to see the disciplinary (and institutional) limitations within which I was working when I wrote this text. In a recently published chapter, "The Responsibility and Limits of Military Chaplains as Public Theologians" (in *Religious Studies Scholars as Public Intellectuals*, Routledge, 2018), I have begun to chart a course toward a more robust dialogue between pastoral theology and theological ethics around the moral decisions that send soldiers to war as well as the moral injuries and confusion that they come home with. This book is what cracked open that door for me and I anticipate my next project will be a more thorough treatment of this relationship.

I have had the honor of performing many funerals for veterans, from World War II to our present conflicts. Precious few World War II veterans now remain alive. My own grandfather died three years ago. Most Vietnam veterans are now in retirement and yet, like my grandfather, many still wrestle with what they endured, what they did, and what it all means. My own generation has now come of age in this time of endless war and so few know the true cost. I pray this book will be of some good to those who care for those who do.

This book could not have been brought to completion without the help of many good people along the way. My gratitude begins with the men and women of 1st Battalion, 320th Field Artillery Regiment. Serving with the "Top Guns" remains the highest honor I have ever—and daresay ever will—know. This project initially began as my Doctor of Ministry dissertation at Erskine Seminary in a program that was sponsored by the United States Army Medical Command. At Erksine, I am deeply grateful to Robin Broome. She was responsive, accommodating, and ensured I had everything I needed to be successful. Along the way, she became a friend. Richard Burnett, my advisor, has been an incredible conversation partner and source of encouragement. He is a living theological treasure. His knowledge of Karl Barth and the Reformed tradition is encyclopedic and his care and precision with theological language has pointed me back to the Christological center on many occasions. He has shepherded me and this project from the inchoate ramblings I mustered during our first meeting to the form my thoughts have taken here. Any theological clarity found within these pages is owed to him and any confusion or error remains my own.

At Richard's insistence, I shared this work with Deborah Hunsinger. I will remain indebted to Deborah for a lifetime. I regret I never had the pleasure of taking a course with her during my time at Princeton Seminary. I am making up for it now. I would be remiss if I did not also mention my beloved professor Robert Dykstra. He is a creative and compassionate pastoral thinker. He has been a continued source of encouragement and it is with his nudge that I step now into further study. My sincere thanks also to Ryan LaMothe (my one and only academic Ranger buddy) who read several chapters and provided many helpful notes. Warren Kinghorn, Amy Laura Hall, and Ross Wagner all have my gratitude for their interest in my work and their efforts to make space for it at Duke.

I am incredibly thankful for my home congregation, Holmdel United Church of Christ. They sent me into military ministry and spiritually sustained me while I was deployed. They are forever beloved to me—especially Rusty Eidmann-Hicks, Susan Muhler, Don Pope, Trish and Landy Gilbert, and the youth group circa 2006-2009. I am grateful to Stephen Boyd, the United Church of Christ endorser for military chaplains. He has been an incredible source of support and a gracious conversation partner on this and many other projects. I am also appreciative of the feedback of my fellow army chaplains and want to thank, in particular, Nick Stavlund and Lucas Rees for their review of this manuscript. I am grateful, too, for my chaplain assistant Heather Rushfeldt for her review and comments on this work and conversations on the Holy Spirit and the presence of God. Jeff Thornberg deserves my utmost thanks for reading and commenting on this text, letting me share some of these insights with Holy Trinity during Lent, and for being my pastor.

Words cannot express my gratitude for John Berardi. He is a faithful friend who was there for me before, during, and after, even when it was not pretty. Likewise, I must thank Michael O'Rourke for his devoted friendship and endless support of my quixotic pursuits. Finally, I must thank Meegan, my wife. We endured together, even if sometimes alone, the trauma of Good Friday, the silence of Holy Saturday, and she is one from whom I learn resurrection hope daily.

    Adam D. Tietje
    Doctor of Theology Student
    Duke University Divinity School
    Durham, North Carolina

*1*

# War Is Hell. Coming Home Is Hell, Too.

In *Packing Inferno*, Iraq War veteran Tyler Boudreau describes his experience going to war and coming home. He writes:

> They say war is hell, but I say it's the foyer to hell. I say coming home is hell, and hell ain't got no coordinates. You can't find it on the charts, because there are no charts. Hell is no place at all, so when you're there, you're nowhere—you're lost. The narrative, that's your chart, your own story. There are guys who come home from war and live fifty years without a narrative, fifty years lost. They don't even know their own story, never have, and never will. But they're moving amidst the text every day and every long night without even realizing it. . . . They live inside the narrative like a cell, and their only escape is to understand its dimensions.[1]

It has been said that "war is hell" and it is, but, as Tyler Boudreau suggests, so is coming home.[2] Combat veterans come home from war with deep psychological and spiritual wounds.[3] These wounds

---

1. Boudreau, *Packing Inferno*, quoted in Brock and Lettini, *Soul Repair*, 65.

2. This quote is commonly attributed to William Sherman. He may have used it in conversation, but there is no written record. Its origins are uncertain.

3. The term veteran is often used to mean those who have left active service. By combat veteran, I mean those who have gone to war and come home,

are related to their combat story, their ability to give voice to it, and, as Boudreau suggests, their ability to "understand its dimensions." Therefore, it is useful to begin this study on the care of the spiritual wounds of war with a short summary of the narrative that underlies what is not simply an interest in undertaking it but an overwhelming necessity. As will be seen, telling our stories—in the presence of God and one another—is to begin to find our way home from the hell of war. Even more important, though, is to hear the story of God's descent into our hell and his overcoming of it.

With that in mind, this chapter begins with a brief narration of my own story of going to war and coming home. I then move to the task of outlining the shape and form of the spiritual wounds or traumas of war. I offer Luke's parable of the prodigal son stuck in the far country as a useful metaphor for understanding the situation of combat veterans who come home from war. Likewise, on Holy Saturday, Jesus's own far country journey finds its end. On Holy Saturday, God makes his place in the grave alongside all who suffer. The church, her pastors, and all those who seek to care for those who come home from war would do well to hear this story anew. Therefore, this chapter concludes with the claim that Holy Saturday is the most fitting place to theologically ground the spiritual care of war wounded souls.

## War is Hell.

When I first entered active duty in 2009, I served as a chaplain for a field artillery battalion. Shooting artillery is a highly technical skill that requires real-time calculations and decisions to ensure that mass-casualty producing artillery shells land in the right place at the right time. Many soldiers in my battalion had trained for over a decade to hone their skills. Being an infantry soldier is its own

including active service members. Thus, I often use soldier and veteran interchangeably. Moreover, when I use the term soldiers to refer to the class of those who have gone to war and come home, I mean for these references to be inclusive of all branches of military service, e.g., sailors, airmen, and marines.

unique specialty and also requires extensive training. Six months before we deployed, my soldiers reorganized as provisional infantry squads and platoons and began training for an infantry mission in Afghanistan. For nearly all of them, this was an unwelcome reality. Over time, some learned to "embrace the suck," while others fought it every step of the way.

In the summer of 2010, the very beginning of the "surge" in Afghanistan, our brigade was positioned in forward operating bases and combat outposts along the Arghandab River. We were in the "spiritual heartland" of the Taliban and our mission was to prevent them from overtaking the second most important city in Afghanistan, Kandahar. Enemy personnel, weapons, and equipment were flowing freely when we arrived. Our task was to counter the insurgency by clearing the valley, holding the newly gained ground, and then maintaining order to facilitate the rebuilding of communities.

It was truly a baptism by fire. When we arrived to our area of operations (AO), the infantry company our battalion was replacing had already taken heavy casualties. Two more of their soldiers were killed while they introduced us to the key community leaders, terrain features, and tactics necessary to survive what we found to be a veritable mine field.[4] Our AO was the fertile soil along the Arghandab River. Fed with water diverted from the river into canals and irrigation ditches, it was lush with grape vineyards and pomegranate orchards, along with marijuana and poppy fields. I was told by one of the locals that when early Muslim traders arrived to this valley, they believed they had rediscovered the Garden of Eden.

Sown in the soil were also countless improvised explosive devices (IEDs). Most were built to detonate when a pressure sensitive plate was stepped on, closing a simple circuit, and detonating

---

4. See Mockenhaupt, "The Last Patrol," for a close look at our transition with a unit from the 82nd Airborne Division. His article describes the very last patrol conducted by one of their platoons with one of ours. I took part in this mission, although I moved with a different element. I can personally attest to much of what Mockenhaupt reports.

buried mortar rounds or homemade explosives (HME). While the pomegranates were supposedly the best in the world, HME was the main export when we arrived. The Taliban had expelled the locals and established HME factories in the now abandoned villages. They prevented the farmers from harvesting their fields and getting their goods to market. The farmers took refuge in larger towns on the edge of the desert and the landowners that could afford it sought safety in Kandahar.

The day my battalion assumed responsibility from that warweary company of paratroopers, we received our first significant casualties. In less than ten minutes, three soldiers from Alpha Battery had stepped on IEDs, all of them with traumatic amputations of their lower extremities. One—who had been nearly cut in half—died in the helicopter on the way to the hospital, only to be revived when he got there.

That day—July 12, 2010—was the first of many that led me to increasingly wonder if I—if we—would ever make it home. Even if we did, could we ever be the same, physically, psychologically, or spiritually? Two days later, a sniper shot one of our soldiers in the head while he was standing guard in one of the towers at Alpha Battery's combat outpost.[5] The bullet went through his helmet, his skull, his brain, and lodged itself on the other side of the helmet. I'll never forget the way his body bounced on the litter as they took him toward the gate or the mess of blood, bone, and brain that resulted from the devastating force of the bullet's impact. The medics continued to try to get him breathing, if only to show us that they were doing everything they could. As they worked, I prayed the only prayers I could muster.

His platoon sergeant had sent him to see me before we deployed. He was afraid of dying. I tried to normalize his fear. I told him, "We're all afraid." It seemed that it was different for him. He went absent without leave (AWOL) a few days later. The platoon sergeant called his mother. He must have told her that her son talked to me. She wanted to know what I thought. Over the phone,

---

5. See Taylor, "Death Comes," for reporting on this incident and the challenges our battalion faced as we began our mission.

I could tell she was a religious woman and she wanted her son to do the right thing. "He was nervous about deploying," was all I said by way of describing our conversation. She seemed to know more than she let on: "I told him we're all going to die one day, each one of us. You just have to trust in God. When it's your time to go there's nothing you can do to stop it." He came back a few days before we deployed. Perhaps he had had a genuine premonition of his own death. No one else had come to me with quite the same fear. I don't think I'll ever comprehend the courage that must have taken. The only certainty seemed to be, "There's nothing you can do to stop it."[6]

Trauma, guilt, grief, and fear all mounted for me and my soldiers as the summer slowly and painfully wore on. There was IED blast after IED blast. Many escaped with only minor wounds. But as time wore on, there were dozens of traumatic amputations from IEDs and more deaths.

July 30th was the next devastating milestone for our battalion. What started as a forty-eight-hour mission turned into a bloody battle that lasted for days. We fought to keep control of a small patch of blood-stained earth at a key intersection initially known as objective Bakersfield. Many IEDs were found and safely destroyed. Three were not and two more soldiers were killed, another had his foot amputated, and many others were wounded. The next day, I walked down to objective Bakersfield to check on my soldiers.[7] I had already seen the death and despair in the eyes

---

6. These conversations are documented in my unpublished account of our deployment, "Faith and Doubt."

7. For an account of the Bakersfield operation see Broadwell, *All In*. Our battalions efforts were featured prominently in her book about David Petraeus's leadership in Afghanistan. While the book was clouded in controversy after news of their affair broke, her sections on 1st Battalion, 320th Field Artillery Regiment are a much appreciated record of what my soldiers did and endured in Afghanistan. By way of capturing a bit of personal history, I met Broadwell while she was in our AO, doing interviews with our commander and others. My commander suggested that she interview me, given my breadth of experience with our soldiers and across the battlefield. It is probably just as well that the interview never happened.

of those who had rotated out. Those who stayed could no longer keep their hands from shaking. The combat and traumatic stress were overwhelming. They had hardly slept and, if they did, it was in foxholes they had dug in the dusty earth.

I am not sure I truly knew fear until I knew it that day and the next. Even though we had the close air support provided by the Kiowa and Apache helicopters overhead, we continued to take fire. The Taliban eventually got their rifle-mounted grenade launcher zeroed-in on our position. For over an hour, we took a beating. I ran from casualty to casualty trying to provide comfort to the wounded and assistance to the medics. The next day, it was more of the same, except that I, too, became a casualty. It was just a few small pieces of shrapnel scattered across my body. I did not even fully realize what had happened at the time. The previous blast had badly wounded my first sergeant and I was busy trying to get him to cover. When the dust settled that day and I finally laid down on my sleeping bag, the flashbacks kept coming as my body involuntarily recoiled at the reliving of each shock. I am not sure how I ever made it to sleep that night.

In the first three months, seven soldiers were killed from our small artillery battalion, dozens experienced traumatic amputations from IED explosions, and a full 20 percent were awarded the Purple Heart for wounds received in combat. All the while, I performed regular services of Word and Sacrament, prayed with soldiers, counseled soldiers, conducted traumatic event debriefings, and honored each one of our fallen soldiers with memorial ceremonies. When one of our soldiers was cut in two by an IED, I went to minister to his platoon, but I confess to only being able to go through the motions one more time. I was hiding symptoms of post-traumatic stress, experiencing compassion fatigue, and had nothing left to give. It was all I could do to hang on for the few more days until I went on leave. I wrote about this during my deployment:

> My first stop at Kandahar Airfield on my way out of country for much-needed leave was the chapel. I went

seeking some sense of God's presence. It was dark outside when I entered the dimly lit sanctuary. I was aghast as I walked past all the books, pamphlets, and bibles available in the foyer. I looked around at the wooden sanctuary, complete with pews and stained glass windows, and my initial instinct was anger and then jealousy. I breathed them out and kept searching the room with my eyes, slowly, carefully. On a little table before going down the center aisle, there on the left side I spotted a small journal with a photograph of Mother Teresa on the cover. I knew immediately it was there for me. I picked one up, flipped to the article, and began to read. I learned about some recently published letters and personal writings in which it became evident that this deeply spiritual woman had struggled for decades with a profound sense of the absence of God. "I have come to love the darkness for I believe now that it is a part, a very, very, small part of Jesus's darkness and pain on earth." As I read those words I laid down my burden and wept.[8]

In this quote, I found the hope I needed to keep going. In my experience of God-abandonment, in the midst of great suffering and evil, I found strength in knowing that Christ, too, suffered pain and darkness such that now all suffering is bound and contained by his own and through which his love can be known.

It was surreal to see tracer rounds being shot below me as I left our AO in a Blackhawk helicopter and then, a few days later, to be sitting in my own home. There, I spent time with my wife, performed my sister's wedding, and visited with family and friends. I was even able to visit several of my wounded soldiers at Walter Reed Army Medical Center in Washington, D.C. I never adjusted to being home. How could anyone when, all the while, you knew you had to go back?

When I returned to Afghanistan, everything had changed. After taking so many casualties, my commander finally received permission to undertake a devastating offensive. The abandoned

8. Tietje, "Faith and Doubt." The quote from Mother Teresa is found in Teresa, *Come Be My Light*, 241.

villages the Taliban used as HME factories and safe houses were too well defended and booby trapped with IEDs. The only way beyond the impasse was to destroy the villages. To be clear, the residents had long since abandoned their homes. They were now only used as strongholds by the Taliban.[9] When the bombs began to fall, the Taliban realized that the rules of the game had fundamentally changed and the fighters left the valley—at least until the next fighting season. Fighting season. It sounds strange but, just like a sport, fighting has a season in Afghanistan. It picks up in the spring, with the opening of the mountain passes from Pakistan, the coming of warmer nights, and the concealment of vegetation. It tapers off as the nights cool, the leaves fall, and the mountain passes become impassible. The Taliban's early withdrawal allowed me to focus on caring for my soldiers and eased my overwhelming anxiety.

After the Taliban retreated, we were able to freely patrol the entire valley, all the way to the river. One of the most important symbols of our progress was having the privilege of baptizing one of my soldiers in the Arghandab River. Unfortunately, a few weeks later and a few hundred meters from where my soldier publicly bore witness to his faith in Christ, there were several more IED blasts that would kill another soldier and cause two more traumatic amputations.

A few weeks earlier, I remember several of those soldiers grimly joking that any one of us would be lucky to leave with an amputation; at least he would leave alive. This sort of gallows humor was pervasive and helped us cope with the nearness of death. By the time we redeployed back to the United States, the rebuilding of the destroyed villages had begun, with the mosques being constructed first. Farmers were once again allowed to freely work

---

9. News of the destruction of these villages was widely reported and widely criticized. As someone who walked through each of those villages in the aftermath, watched as they were rebuilt, and witnessed the renewal of life among the residents of the valley afterward, I tend to side with my commander's decision. See Ackerman, "25 Tons of Bombs," and Ackerman, "Why I Flattened," for my commander's rebuttal.

in their fields, vineyards, and orchards, and, with the coming of spring, it seemed for a moment that hope, too, had returned.

## Coming Home is Hell, Too.

I was still on post-deployment leave when I received the call telling me that one of my soldiers had died of an overdose. It was a cruel bookend to the deployment. Two months before we left for Afghanistan, one of my fellow staff officers had shot himself in the head. The first few weeks back at the office were eerily quiet, and then the dam broke. In story after story, I recognized myself.

My soldiers and I, too, struggled to find meaning and purpose in the aftermath of war. A large number of them suffered the symptoms of posttraumatic stress disorder (PTSD) in silence and self-medicated with alcohol or drugs. The ones that did seek help found our behavioral health system incredibly overloaded. It took weeks to get an appointment. Many gave up seeking help in frustration and joined their peers in self-medication. Depression, despair, and thoughts of suicide were commonplace. Soldier after soldier was punished for misconduct and many were separated from service.[10] Within six months of coming home, four soldiers had killed themselves. We had found our way home, but we were still lost. I spoke to this reality at the memorial ceremony of the second of my soldiers who died at his own hands when our battalion returned home from southern Afghanistan.

---

10. Some misconduct could easily be attributed to negative coping with trauma and the effects of war. Many alcohol-related incidents were simply the result of self-medication gone awry. In addition to any negative coping with war, a number of other unfortunate factors came together during the service of many of my soldiers. The "surges" in both Afghanistan and Iraq required the retention of soldiers whose misconduct would have otherwise demanded separation. Additionally, the bar for entry into service was lowered by the granting of tens of thousands of waivers for soldiers to enlist with misdemeanors, felonies, and histories of significant drug and alcohol abuse. This also coincided with the significant economic downturn of late 2008. See the 2010 report by the Army, "Health Promotion," 69.

> Brothers and sisters, we may be home from the war, but the war has come home with us. Of all we have had to fear, and there has been much, this scares us most. For if not at home, where is peace to be found? And yet it is here at home in the silence of our thoughts that the voices of our guilt and grief have cried out the loudest. Peace, we have learned, is not as easy as getting on a plane. Memories forever burned into our minds and bodies threaten to take us back daily and lead us to wonder if our most difficult days may yet come. Whereas once we faced the enemy with our squads and platoons, now it seems we fight on alone. With the Psalmist we cry out, "Surely the darkness shall cover me, and the light around me become night" (Ps 139:11).[11]

Sergeant Justin Junkin had been drinking alone, reminiscing about a dear friend who was killed in combat. Overwhelmed with emotion, he loaded his pistol and killed himself with his wife and child asleep in the next room.

I served to minister to such soul wounds the best I was able, even as I, too, was lost and hurting after coming home. I read Scripture and prayed every day while I was deployed. Toward the end, it became almost unbearable. When I returned home, I stopped praying for months and questioned my calling. I was angry at God. I was not only grief-stricken for my soldiers but also for myself. At the height of my depression, during the summer of 2011, I visited my home congregation to thank them for their love and support during the deployment. Their cards and letters were truly life-sustaining. I will never forget what one of these faithful women told me when I confessed that I was not praying. She said, "It's okay. You don't have to pray right now. We are praying on your behalf." I'll never forget that. It was one of the most important things anyone could have said to me at that point. It still speaks volumes to me about the nature of the church at prayer on behalf of a world that cannot pray for itself.

---

11. Tietje, "Home from the War."

As I slowly reconnected with the life of the church at prayer and continued to journey with my soldiers who had been so spiritually devastated by war, I came to a renewed understanding of my calling. I was later reassigned to a Warrior Transition Battalion (WTB), a unit that focuses exclusively on the healing of soldiers who are wounded, ill, or injured. Less than 10 percent of my WTB soldiers had been wounded in combat action, but a full third of them have been diagnosed with PTSD. In this setting, I worked with soldiers on a daily basis who struggle with the spiritual wounds of war after coming home.

My story continues to unfold, but this much is clear: I now understand my calling to be, in part, directed toward the care of those who have been spiritually wounded in combat. I see this book as an important part of that work. I pray that it might be of some good to the ministry of the church, pastors, chaplains, and anyone else who cares for those who wrestle with the horrors of war after coming home.

## The Spiritual Wounds of War

The Greek root of the word trauma simply means wound. Throughout this study, I will be using trauma and wound interchangeably. In her groundbreaking study, *Trauma and Recovery*, psychiatrist Judith Herman defines psychological trauma as:

> An affliction of the powerless. At the moment of trauma, the victim is rendered helpless by overwhelming force. When the force is that of nature, we speak of disasters. When the force is that of other human beings, we speak of atrocities. Traumatic events overwhelm the ordinary systems of care that give people a sense of control, connection, and meaning.[12]

This overwhelming event is most often an encounter with death or its possibility, an all too frequent occurrence in combat. The result of this overwhelming force is that the traumatic returns

12. Herman, *Trauma and Recovery*, 33.

in the form of intrusive thoughts, daytime hallucinations, and nightmares—among many other frightful symptoms. As a result, hyper-vigilance becomes a way of life for the traumatized. The survivor of trauma makes every effort to avoid triggers that might provoke a painful re-experiencing of the event and negative emotional reactions. These are the symptomatic responses to trauma that can lead to a diagnosis of PTSD: re-experiencing the traumatic event (e.g., intrusive thoughts, distressing dreams), avoiding stimuli related to the trauma, "negative alterations in cognitions and mood," and increased arousal (hyper-vigilance).[13] While experiencing these symptoms, the survivor of trauma may have a particularly difficult time maintaining her significant relationships with loved ones and even herself.

Of considerable concern for us, those who have endured significant trauma often wonder if God has abandoned them. Herman writes:

> Traumatic events call into question basic human relationships. They breach the attachments of family, friendship, love, and community. They shatter the construction of the self that is formed and sustained in relation to others. *They undermine the belief systems that give meaning to human experience. They violate the victim's faith in a*

---

13. *DSM-V*, 271. While the *DSM-V* suggests four primary components to the disorder: re-experiencing painful memories (criterion B), effortful avoidance of trauma cues (criterion C), negative changes in mood and perception (criterion D), and increased arousal (criterion E), in a 2010 study, Engdahl et al. found that "observed differences in neuronal interactions reflect the re-experiencing component" (Engdahl et al., "Post-traumatic Stress," 6). The implication is that avoidance, negative emotions, and increased arousal may simply be derivative of the re-experiencing aspect of PTSD. They connect their findings to studies on the "effects of electrical stimulation of the cortex during brain surgery, namely the elicitation of reliving or re-enacting past experiences. . . . These re-enactments are evocative of the flashbacks experienced by patients suffering from PTSD" (Engdahl et al., "Post-traumatic Stress," 6). Perhaps just as remarkable is the fact that these effects, while attenuated, were also observed in subjects in remission. Also of note, the *DSM-V* does include emotions of guilt and shame, a nod to some of the concerns noted by the clinicians who have called for a recognition of moral injury (see *DSM-V*, 275).

> *natural or divine order and cast the victim into a state of existential crisis.*[14]

Trust in the nature of God and reality can be shattered by traumatic events and there is often a loss of meaning, purpose, and hope. God's justice and God's love can both be put on trial in the wake of horrific trauma. As a result, the traumatized often feel cut off from God with no hope of return. This experience of God-forsakenness can cut deep into the soul of veterans.

While trauma is a fear-based stress reaction to an encounter with death or its possibility, the reality that clinicians are now uncovering is that many soldiers coming home from Afghanistan and Iraq have exhibited symptoms of PTSD that have nothing to do with feeling powerless or fearing imminent death but rather with acts that violate their conscience, e.g., the killing of innocents.[15] The startling reality is that the greatest predictor of PTSD symptoms among combat veterans is killing. The research consistently bears out that the perpetration of violence is more injurious to soldiers than simply witnessing it. One study suggests that "actual killing or not acting to prevent killing better predicted higher suicidality, more PTSD symptoms, and other mental health disorders."[16]

As a result, many psychologists have begun setting out criteria and treatment modalities for what has come to be known as moral injury. Litz et al. define moral injury as "perpetrating, failing to prevent, or bearing witness to acts that transgress deeply held moral beliefs and expectations."[17] Or, as Rita Brock and Gabriella Lettini put it in their book *Soul Repair: Recovering From Moral Injury After War*, moral injury follows from "having transgressed one's basic moral identity and violated core moral beliefs."[18] While clinical research is in its infancy—the first comprehensive study

14. Herman, *Trauma and Recovery*, 51, emphasis added.
15. *DSM-V*, 274–76.
16. Worthington and Langberg, "Religious Considerations," 276.
17. Litz et al., "Moral Injury," 697.
18. Brock and Lettini, *Soul Repair*, xiv.

was only completed in 2009[19]—moral injury is as old as war itself and is evident in Homer's epics.[20] Responses to moral injury include guilt, shame, depression, and feelings of worthlessness, despair, and remorse. Many veterans are explicit in the use of theological language to describe these experiences and God's judgment figures prominently.

Even though it is clinicians who have largely taken the lead in understanding moral injury and prescribing treatment, it should be evident that moral injury is also a spiritual wound. Both PTSD and moral injury have psychological and spiritual aspects. More clarity is necessary to understand the relationship between the different perspectives that psychology and theology bring to bear on these "invisible" wounds of war. This clarity may be found in chapter 3 with the help of Deborah Hunsinger's use of Karl Barth's "Chalcedonian pattern" to relate theological and psychological concepts.[21] For now, this much is clear: in the aftermath of war, many veterans return with their faith shattered. The hellish realities of combat persist in very real ways, even though the soldier has come home. These hellish realities—encounters with death, moral failures, and seemingly unending grief—may inflict deep spiritual wounds that leave many feeling abandoned by God or judged unworthy to enter into his presence.

## A Far Country Journey

In Luke 15, Jesus tells the parable of a son who is stuck in a far country. Reduced to poverty by his previously prodigal ways, the son remains in the far country, in servitude and filth, to survive. I find here a metaphor for the situation in which combat veterans

---

19. See Litz et al., "Moral Injury," 695–706.

20. Jonathan Shay does an excellent job of bringing the wisdom of those ancient epics into our own time in both *Achilles in Vietnam*, which draws on the stories of the *Iliad*, and *Odysseus in America*, which draws on the stories of the *Odyssey*. In fact, it is Shay who first uses the term moral injury to describe the moral betrayal of soldiers by their leaders in combat in *Achilles in Vietnam*.

21. See also Hunsinger, *Pastoral Counseling*.

find themselves.[22] In the aftermath of morally troubling and traumatic combat experiences, they, too, remain stuck in a far country, often struggling just to survive. On the other side of trauma, one's sense of purpose, meaning, and faith are often badly damaged or destroyed. What remains for the combat veteran in this far-country dislocation?

Karl Barth outlines the obedience of Christ as Son in the incarnation as "The Way of the Son of God into the Far Country."[23] With the help of Barth's heading, we see that the incarnation turns the parable of the disobedient son on its head. It is as an obedient Son to the Father that Christ empties himself of his heavenly glory and makes his way to our far country. The Son of God willingly suffered this dislocation in the far country even unto death on a cross and descent into the very depths of hell.[24] In Jesus's parable, it is the love and mercy of the father that remains for the prodigal son. This is the upshot of Hans Urs von Balthasar's interpretation of Holy Saturday. Even as Jesus experiences God's utter abandonment on the cross and descends into hell, through the Holy Spirit,

---

22. It is important to note that this metaphor does not illuminate all who go to war and come home. It is also important to note, I do not mean for any judgment of the prodigal son's agency in the parable to be broadly applicable to the agency of combat veterans in general. The prodigal chooses to demand his inheritance and leave his father for the far country. While soldiers in America's current volunteer army choose to join, this has not always been nor may it always be the case. Further, this study makes no judgment of such a choice. Ultimately, my interest in the parable lies in where the son ends up—the far country. How soldiers end up there may be the result of their own agency (e.g., an explicit war crime), or may be the result of circumstances far beyond their choosing (e.g., an ambush set by the enemy).

23. See Barth, *CD*, 4.1:157–210.

24. Jesus goes to the far country *pro nobis*. I do not mean to suggest that American soldiers are sent to the far country on a divine mission. By setting Jesus's far country journey alongside the far country journey of soldiers, some may be tempted to think the far country analogy runs both ways. It does not. I am in no way endorsing a theology of empire. Indeed, I suspect that, for some, moral injury actually occurs at the intersection of the demands of the "liturgy of war" of American civil religion and the demands of religious faith. For more on the "liturgy of war," see Hauerwas, *War and the American Difference*.

the love of the Father for the Son remains.[25] Thus, veterans may know that, even in the farthest reaches of the far country, even in the depths of hell, God has already made his place with them.

In this book, I posit that the heart of the Easter Triduum, Holy Saturday, is a fruitful place to begin a theological exploration of this far country dislocation and what might remain for combat veterans who come home spiritually wounded. In what follows, I begin to probe toward a pastoral theology of Holy Saturday and the shape of pastoral care for those who come home from war spiritually wounded. I suggest that this theology be grounded in Christ's own far country dislocation, which begins with the incarnation and traces through to the very depths of hell. The upshot, I hope, is a pastoral response to the spiritual wounds of war that is grounded in the trinitarian relationship of the divine persons and draws those who suffer back into communion with the one God.

With that in view, in chapter 2, I suggest that the church embrace a theology of Holy Saturday, particularly in light of the church's confession of Jesus's descent into hell. In this vein, I examine the catholic creeds, as well as the witness of Reformation era confessions and catechisms surrounding Jesus's descent. Calvin locates the descent with Jesus's cry of dereliction. Calvin's pastoral wisdom—that the God-abandonment of Jesus on the cross is a message of great comfort, especially to those feel that they, too, have been abandoned by God—remains central to my constructive efforts. His doctrine of the descent is brought forward with the help of Karl Barth. In conversation with Hans Urs von Balthasar, Barth's doctrine of the descent and the God-abandonment of Jesus is extended from the cross to include the grave. I conclude that the story of salvation—and even God's very being as God for us and with us as Father, Son, and Holy Spirit—turns on this moment in the life of God, that is, in which God abandons God on the cross and in the grave. Indeed, it is from this moment of utter hopelessness that our salvation and all hope spring forth.

---

25. Balthasar, *Mysterium Paschale*, 148–81.

In chapter 3, a particular way of understanding how to relate theological doctrine with psychological theory is set forth. In order to lay the groundwork for understanding trauma and moral injury, not simply as psychological damage but also as soul wounds, we need to elucidate the differences between psychological trauma and spiritual anguish. While the two conditions often appear in the suffering of a single individual, it is important to differentiate between them and not confuse them with each other. In her book, *Theology and Pastoral Counseling: A New Interdisciplinary Approach*, Deborah van Deusen Hunsinger takes up the question of how to properly distinguish and relate psychological conceptual frameworks and theological frameworks of understanding. Drawing on Karl Barth as well as the work of her husband, George Hunsinger, Deborah Hunsinger develops a critical and constructive proposal for relating psychological and spiritual issues that will provide a method for illuminating the plight of soldiers returning from war.

Developing and applying what she calls a "Chalcedonian pattern thought" to the dialogue between theology and psychology, Hunsinger's use of Barth is helpful.[26] The criteria she develops will be explained in chapter 3 and then applied to the work of theologian Shelly Rambo, in her book, *Spirit and Trauma: A Theology of Remaining*. When Rambo's argument is examined in light of the "Chalcedonian" criteria developed by Hunsinger, it becomes clear that Rambo's way of articulating the gospel in light of trauma theory essentially disfigures the promises and claims of the gospel. Because Rambo makes her substantive theological points within an essentially psychological framework (the lens of trauma theory), the robust good news proclaimed in the resurrection is severely attenuated. Gaining clarity about why it is important to not, on the one hand, separate theological from psychological thinking, nor, on the other, to confuse these conceptual worlds, while placing psychology within a larger spiritual framework of meaning—all of these important moves will be explicated by Hunsinger's use of

---

26. See Hunsinger, *Pastoral Counseling*.

# Toward A Pastoral Theology of Holy Saturday

Barth's thoroughly Chalcedonian imagination. While some of this may appear technical, it is the conceptual linchpin of the book's argument: namely, to gain clarity about the role of pastors and chaplains in seeking to provide spiritual sustenance to soldiers returning from the chaos and terror of war.

Chapter 4 traces the shape pastoral care might take for spiritually-wounded combat veterans. Judith Herman's stages of recovery—safety, remembrance and mourning, and reconnection—provide a helpful framework.[27] Indeed, both the psychological healing of PTSD and healing of moral injury are signs that point us toward spiritual healing, that is, salvation. Balthasar's Holy Saturday theology is the backdrop for a conversation between Herman's work and Jesus's parable of the prodigal son. The fruit of this interplay is that sanctuary, lament and confession, and forgiveness and reconciliation provide a trajectory for the pastoral care of the spiritual wounds of war. I will argue that pastoral care for the spiritual wounds of war entails offering sanctuary, giving voice to lament and confession, and seeking forgiveness and reconciliation. Along the way, I draw spiritual analogies to Herman's psychological framework.

Finally, in chapter 5, I suggest that pastoral caregivers, through prayer, make Holy Saturday their spiritual home. Henri Nouwen's *Wounded Healer* provides a basis and form for such ministry. With Jesus, those who offer care make their place with those who suffer. It is as wounded healers that pastoral caregivers prayerfully offer those who come home from war sanctuary, space for lament and confession, and proclaim God's word of forgiveness. Just as only the welcomed guest can be a gracious host, so too only those who recognize their own wounds can welcome those for whom they care into the theological space of Holy Saturday.

In the liturgies of the church, Holy Saturday is marked by absence and silence. The altar is stripped bare. The Eucharist does not return until the Easter Vigil. There is no light from candles and no vestments are worn. As the church remembers Jesus's burial

---

27. See Herman, *Trauma and Recovery*, 133–213.

and death, we hold vigil at the tomb and wait. This is where the church—and her pastors and chaplains—must begin with those who come home from war and, indeed, with all those who suffer. The good news of Holy Saturday is that God in Christ came to keep vigil with us all, even in the darkness of a tomb and in the depths of hell. It is to the telling of this Holy Saturday story that we now turn.

## 2

# The Story of Holy Saturday

"My God, my God why have you forsaken me?" In both the gospels of Mark and Matthew these are Jesus's last words. He is quoting Psalm 22: "My God, my God why have you forsaken me? Why are you so far from helping me, from the words of my groaning? O my God, I cry by day, but you do not answer; and by night, but find no rest." There is a great theological debate about what this last utterance signifies, whether despair or faith. Some suggest that having fully taken on the sin of the world, Jesus is indeed Godforsaken. I find it ironic that subsequent Christian martyrs die with such steadfast faith and yet Jesus seems to lose his. Of course, Psalm 22 itself moves from the despair of its opening upward to affirmations of faith and hope. Even in the darkness of that hour, even in the shadow of death, was Jesus holding onto hope?[1]

I PENNED THESE WORDS in the middle of my deployment to Afghanistan. I was trying to understand the trauma that I had experienced in light of the trauma of the cross. On the cross, Christ joins in solidarity with our wounds in all their forms—but where do we turn when we find ourselves on the other side of trauma, on the other side of the encounter with death? Where do we look

1. Tietje, "Faith and Doubt."

for God's presence-in-absence when new life is yet inconceivable and Easter Sunday is still so far away? On the other side of trauma, we may fall into an abyss of God-forsakenness whose limits are known only to the One who has gone before us and the only one who will ever fully plumb its depths.

Only on Holy Saturday does Jesus's cry of dereliction find its full end. Only on Holy Saturday has Christ reached the final destination of his journey into the far country by suffering utter God-abandonment in the depths of hell for us. It is Christ's going to the dead that is the hallmark of God's presence-in-absence. It is the love of Christ as obedient Son that leads him to this limit. It is the love of the Father for his Son that ultimately overcomes it. It is the Spirit that is the Holy Love between them that persists beyond the abyss.

For those who have descended into the abyss, the story of Holy Saturday is a story of hope. Jesus's descent into hell assures us that God's presence abides in the depths. The story of God abandoning God assures us that Jesus has plumbed the depths and goes into the depths with us. Because God has gone into the silence of the grave, the Word of God is spoken even in God's silence. Thus, it is on Holy Saturday that those who experience God-abandonment in the far country may encounter the Spirit of Love that yet remains and, with this encounter, begin their journey home. In this chapter, we will examine what it means to speak of Holy Saturday as the story of God.

## Creeds, Confessions, and Catechisms

Evangelical theologians Wayne Grudem and John Piper have been outspoken in their repudiation of the notion that Christ descended to hell. They reject the *descensus ad inferna* (descended into hell) clause of the *Apostles' Creed*, arguing that it is of dubious historical origins and lacks clear scriptural warrant.[2] Catholic theologian Martin Connell agrees but also argues that *descensus ad inferna*

---

2. Lauber, *Barth on the Descent*, 76–77.

is simply a corruption of the older tradition of *descensus ad inferos* (descent to the dead). This older tradition of a "descent to the dead" finds widespread citation in the early Fathers. He argues this point to suggest that we might still affirm Christ's solidarity with us in death without the soteriological questions that are raised by a descent to hell (*ad inferna*).³ For Connell, the theology implicit in the *ad inferna* reading is that sinners who die separated from God's grace can be reconciled. He understands the original theological thrust of the *ad inferos* to be that "the embrace of God's grace is so wide and generous that even the dead get a second chance at salvation."⁴

The "three ecumenical creeds" of the West do not speak with one voice on the question of the descent. In the extant Latin manuscripts for the *Apostles' Creed*, there is attestation for both *ad inferna* and *ad inferos*, with *ad inferna* being the dominant and preferred reading.⁵ The *Nicene Creed* makes no reference to the descent. The *Athanasian Creed*, a much later document, testifies to the *ad inferna* reading.⁶ The *Apostles' Creed*, *Nicene Creed*, and *Athanasian Creed* are accepted by the Roman Catholic Church as well as by Lutherans. Indeed, they are included in the *Book of Concord*.⁷ The *Athanasian Creed* is not, however, taken up by Calvin, Zwingli, or later Reformed divines.⁸ While referred to as "ecumenical" creeds, both the *Apostles' Creed* and the *Athanasian Creed* are used almost exclusively in the West. Of course, the *Nicene Creed*, as professed in the West, includes the controversial *filioque* (and the son) clause that was never accepted in the East.⁹

---

3. Connell, "Descensus Christi," 262–82.

4. Connell, "Descensus Christi," 271.

5. Pelikan and Hotchkiss, *Creeds and Confessions*, 1:669.

6. Pelikan and Hotchkiss, *Creeds and Confessions*, 1:676.

7. Kolb and Wengert, *The Book of Concord*, 19–21.

8. Pelikan and Hotchkiss, *Creeds and Confessions*, 1:673.

9. The *Athanasian Creed* was composed in Latin and was not the product of Athanasius of Alexandria. It also includes a form of the *filioque*. For more on these three creeds, see Pelikan and Hotchkiss, *Creeds and Confessions*, 1:665.

Despite these creedal differences, the descent into hell in both the Roman Catholic and Eastern Orthodox traditions is broadly similar, being understood primarily as a triumphant "harrowing of hell." 1 Peter 3:19 is cited to support Christ preaching to the dead. Images of Jesus breaking the gates of hell to overthrow the powers of evil and Christ preaching to the dead are widespread in Eastern and Western iconography.[10] In the East, this harrowing motif is exemplified in Metrophanes Critopoulos's *Confession of Faith* (1625). The reasons for the descent in his confession are twofold: "to triumph over his enemy the rebel tyrant" and "so that he might release from bondage and affliction those who were held there for the sin of our forefather, and teach them about himself."[11]

Martin Luther, John Calvin, and other Reformers appropriated the "ecumenical" creeds, especially the *Apostles' Creed* into their confessions and catechisms. Both Luther's *Small Catechism* (1529) and the *Large Catechism* (1529) teach Christ's descent into hell as part of the second article of faith. The emphasis in the *Small Catechism* is on deliverance from the powers of death and the devil.[12] This theme is expanded in the *Large Catechism* where Christ "snatches us . . . from the jaws of hell."[13] The *Augsburg Confession* of 1530 also teaches the descent.[14]

In a 1532 Holy Saturday *hauspostille* or "house sermon," Luther preaches at length on the descent. He endorses the imaginative efforts of the iconographers and their portrayal of Christ victoriously breaking the gates of hell and binding the devil. He believes that the childlike simplicity of these images is the closest we can get in this life to understanding what happens between cross and

---

10. Examples of "harrowing of hell" iconography are abound in the East (see Dionysius, *Descent into Hell*) but also appear in the West (see Bermejo, *Christ Leading*).

11. Pelikan and Hotchkiss, *Creeds and Confessions*, 1:502.

12. Pelikan and Hotchkiss, *Creeds and Confessions*, 2:37.

13. Kolb and Wengert, *The Book of Concord*, 434.

14. Pelikan and Hotchkiss, *Creeds and Confessions*, 2:60.

resurrection.¹⁵ He shrewdly anticipates much of the debate in the twentieth and twenty-first centuries, stating:

> Thus, in reference to this article, the world comes and asks many useless, futile questions, whether Christ's soul only descended into hell or whether the Godhead went with it; also what he did there, what kind of resistance the devils offered, and how he overcame them. Then, after they have raised a lot of questions, they conclude, Christ died on the cross, his body was laid in the grave, his soul is in heaven with the Father to whom he commended it, so how then can it be possible that he descended into hell? And thus, finally, this article is thrown into complete doubt.¹⁶

Here, Luther speaks to both the trinitarian questions the descent raises—does Christ's divinity also descend? What remains of the trinitarian relationship in the descent?—and the sort of reasoning that leads to the disavowal of the doctrine altogether.¹⁷ While Luther rejects these efforts as speculation, he has a clear grasp of what is at stake in affirming the descent or its denial. In the end, he is content to teach the descent in simplicity with an affirmation of the traditional harrowing imagery.

The *Formula of Concord* (1577), the climax of second-generation Lutheran debates, also addresses the question of Christ's descent. It notes the questions that arise with this article, notably: "Did it occur only according to the soul, or only according to the

---

15. Luther, *Complete Sermons*, 5:476–82.

16. Luther, *Complete Sermons*, 5:480.

17. Perhaps Luther's judgment on this chapter would be that it is asking futile questions. I humbly disagree with Luther on this point and think that there is much important theological truth at stake in the descent that Luther is content to bypass. I think that questions about what happens in the life of God on the cross and in the descent are important and their implications far-reaching. Karl Barth and Hans Urs von Balthasar are enlisted for the cause. The detractors of such efforts remain, most notably, Alyssa Pitstick. Her now published dissertation is a tightly-argued analysis that gives credence to Luther's prescience about the doubts that also rise when such questions are asked. See Pitstick, *Light in Darkness*.

deity, or according to body and soul, spiritually or corporeally? Does this article belong to Christ's suffering or to his glorious victory and triumph?"[18] Simple faith is endorsed and reference is made to Luther's Holy Saturday sermon for support. Here, again, the questions that become important in the twentieth and twenty-first centuries are raised.

Calvin's *Institutes of the Christian Religion* (1536) and the *Geneva Catechism* (1542) speak with one voice regarding the descent. It is a notably different and more developed voice than its predecessors. Calvin's engagement with the descent in the *Institutes* dates back to its first edition and is filled out in the subsequent ones. Calvin eschews the mythological imagery that develops around the descent and cuts to the chase about its theological import.[19] The descent is about the atonement. He writes:

> He suffered the death that God, in his wrath, had inflicted upon the wicked! . . . The Creed sets forth what Christ suffered in the sight of men, and then appositely speaks of that invisible and incomprehensible judgment which he underwent in the sight of God in order that we might know not only that Christ's body was given as the price of our redemption, but that he paid a greater and more excellent price in suffering in his soul the terrible torments of a condemned and forsaken man.[20]

He goes on: "And unless his soul shared in the punishment, he would have been the Redeemer of bodies alone."[21] There is clear allusion here to Gregory of Nazianzus's insight that "the unassumed is the unredeemed."[22] In the descent, Jesus suffers in body and soul the judgment of God intended for sinners. The descent into hell is the creedal profession of Jesus's God-abandonment in

---

18. Pelikan and Hotchkiss, *Creeds and Confessions*, 2:195.

19. Taking a swipe at this imagery—and perhaps at Luther's childlike affirmation of it—Calvin writes: "It is childish to enclose the souls of the dead in a prison." See Calvin, *Institutes*, 1:514.

20. Calvin, *Institutes*, 1:516.

21. Calvin, *Institutes*, 1:518.

22. Schaff and Wace, *Nicene and Post-Nicene Fathers*, 439.

judgment on our behalf. He affirms Jesus's "cry of dereliction" as such, suggesting that Jesus's descent begins in Gethsemane with the realization that "he stood accused before God's judgment seat for our sake."[23]

In suggesting that, in the descent, Christ suffers God's wrath on our behalf, Calvin goes beyond the triumphant medieval harrowing imagery that Luther endorses and intimately ties it to Christ's work of atonement on the cross. Calvin limits the judgment endured in the descent to only the human nature of Christ. Jesus's divinity does not suffer, only Jesus's humanity—in body and soul. This is no clearer than in Question 68 of the *Geneva Catechism*. The question is asked and answered this way: "But since he is God himself, how could he be in such dread, as if he were forsaken by God? . . . We must hold that it was according to his *human nature* that he was in that extremity: and that in order to allow this, his deity held itself back a little, as if concealed, that is, did not show its power."[24]

As is evident throughout the *Institutes*, Calvin writes with great pastoral sensitivity. He finds comfort in the doctrine of the descent: "he did not shrink from taking our weakness upon himself. . . . From this also arises the comfort for our anguish and sorrow that the apostle holds out to us: that this Mediator has experienced our weaknesses the better to succor us in our miseries (Heb 4:15)."[25] He has deep sensitivity to the spiritual pain for believers who, like Christ—though perhaps differing in degree and kind—feel God-abandoned. He says, "And surely no more terrible abyss can be conceived than to feel yourself forsaken and estranged from God; and when you call upon him, not to be heard. It is as if God himself had plotted your ruin."[26] I think he also implicitly suggests the form our own response to feeling God-forsaken might take when he writes:

---

23. Calvin, *Institutes*, 1:519.
24. Pelikan and Hotchkiss, *Creeds and Confessions*, 2:328, emphasis added.
25. Calvin, *Institutes*, 1:518.
26. Calvin, *Institutes*, 1:516.

> For feeling himself, as it were, forsaken by God, he did not waver in the least from trust in his goodness. This is proved by that remarkable prayer to God in which he cried out in acute agony: "My God, my God, why hast thou forsaken me?" (Matt 27:46). For even though he suffered beyond measure, he did not cease to call him his God, by whom he cried out that he had been forsaken[27]

Though it goes unsaid by Calvin, it seems that Christians, too, might follow in Christ's path of continuing to trust in God's goodness by crying out to God—even in the face of all manner of suffering that might otherwise undermine such trust. I think Calvin's insights here already put us on a good path as we seek to care for those who feel God-abandoned in the aftermath of trauma and moral injury in combat.

The *Heidelberg Catechism* (1563), with its synthesis of Melanchthonian and Calvinist thought, tends more toward Calvin in question forty-four: "Why is there added: 'He descended to hell'? That in my severest tribulations I may be assured that Christ my Lord has redeemed me from hellish anxieties and torment by the unspeakable anguish, pains, and terrors which he suffered in his soul both on the cross and before."[28] The *Heidelberg Catechism* comes down hard on the side of Calvin's pastoral insight about the comforts provided by the descent while only hinting at the atonement theology that provides firm ground for such comfort. It should also be noted that the *Heidelberg Catechism* locates the descent on Good Friday and cuts the descent out from providing any insight to the theological significance of Holy Saturday.

Thus far, it has been shown that the profession of the descent has been important in both the East and the West, with the "harrowing" interpretation largely holding sway in Catholic and Orthodox circles. The Reformers profess the descent's importance, with Luther content to endorse the "harrowing" imagery. Calvin,

---

27. Calvin, *Institutes*, 1:519–20.

28. Pelikan and Hotchkiss, *Creeds and Confessions*, 2:437. The Scriptures cited by the Heidelberg Catechism for this question are the suffering servant (Isa 53:5) and the cry of dereliction (Matt 27:45–46).

on the other hand, ties the descent to his doctrine of atonement, understanding Christ's suffering in body and soul to be God's wrath and abandonment suffered in our stead. He highlights the pastoral comfort that this doctrine provides to those who, borrowing from the *Heidelberg Catechism*, are in their "severest tribulations."[29] It is Calvin who gives the doctrine of the descent its most significant theological underpinning by tying it to the atonement and it is upon this structure that Karl Barth builds.

## Karl Barth on the Descent

In his 1935 lectures on the dogmatic implications of the *Apostles' Creed*, Karl Barth writes, as clearly as elsewhere, that God's self-revelation in Christ is the sole basis for knowledge of God:

> God's revelation in His Son, so far as we understand by that concretely the—to us quite comprehensible—human existence of Jesus Christ, is, as the second article of the Creed will show us, just as strikingly as in keeping with the New Testament, a way into the *darkness* of God; it is the way of Jesus to Golgotha. If, as such, it is a way into the light of God, and is therefore really God's *revelation*, then that is because this Jesus on "the third day rose again from the dead, He ascended into heaven, and sitteth on the right hand of God." But that is said of Jesus the Crucified. Actually, the hidden God here becomes manifest; we are here led right to the limit of what we can conceive in order that *here* (here, where Jesus Himself cries: "My God, my God, why has Thou forsaken me?") we may catch the words, "Behold, your God!" God the Father, as Father of Jesus Christ, is He Who leads His Son into hell and out again.[30]

This revelation is made manifest in the resurrection only in and through the human life and death of Jesus. God is known as God precisely at the moment of God's darkness and hiddenness on the

---

29. Pelikan and Hotchkiss, *Creeds and Confessions*, 2:437.
30. Barth, *Credo*, 21.

cross in Jesus's cry of dereliction. Here, it is also clear that the relationship between Father and Son is one defined by this journey of descent into the depths of hell. This begs the very questions from which Luther backs away, questions which will subsequently be taken up. Later in the lectures, Barth, following Calvin, relates the descent with the Anselmian atonement tradition. He writes:

> The eternal Word has got to be present in our flesh, that, as it is put in Romans 8:3, "sin may be condemned in the flesh," i.e. that man in all that he is and does may, as sinner, be placed openly and simultaneously in judgment, i.e. under the sentence and punishment of God, and that he may now experience what it means to have forsaken God and therefore in turn to be forsaken by God. The presence of God, and only that, makes the cross the Cross, that is the cursed tree; makes death punishment, that is, righteous and irrevocable retribution; makes the inconceivable way that is to be trodden in death the descent into hell, i.e. the sink into that despair: "My God, my God, why hast Thou forsaken Me?" He, God, makes Him "Who knew no sin" "to be sin" . . . that is, to be one over whom breaks curse, punishment and ordeal.[31]

Here, Barth follows Calvin closely, identifying Jesus's God-forsakenness as precisely the place of God's judgment. It is in his humanity that Jesus identifies with our flesh and indeed takes on our sin as his sin (2 Cor 5:21) and our lot as those who "have forsaken God" in order to be God-forsaken in our stead. The descent into hell is a curse (Gal 3:13), a punishment (Rom 6:23), and a miserable ordeal that God allows Christ to endure. In short, it is the fullness of God's wrath, God's just judgment upon sin. Christ identifies fully with our fate.

In contrast with Calvin, for Barth, it is Jesus's divinity that allows him to be such a one for us. The true depth of sin and death is only revealed through Jesus's suffering and death—that is, with God's identification with our fate. The death, even violent or painful, of a sinless human would not reveal anything about sin and

---

31. Barth, *Credo*, 89–90.

could not be conceived of as uniquely curse, punishment, or ordeal. We can know that hell is the punishment for sinful humanity precisely because this is what Christ himself endured on the cross. The contrast is stark between the Old Testament understanding of "dead souls dwelling in the comfortless yet tolerable wasteland of Sheol" and the New Testament images of the outer darkness, the weeping and gnashing of teeth, and the eternal fire that burns like Gehenna.[32] David Lauber sums up Barth's conception of this difference in the New Testament: "Hell is not introduced because of a pessimistic anthropology or abstract speculation regarding life beyond the grave; rather, hell is an actual threat to sinful humanity because it is the only way of accounting for the torment that Jesus Christ endured in the face of his imminent death."[33]

With Calvin, Barth understands the descent to be interpretive of the atonement accomplished on the cross. He diverges from Calvin (and Anselm) in that this atonement is not simply a vicarious *quid pro quo* act. For Barth, there is no movement of wrath to love as part of a mechanistic exchange paid for with Christ's blood. As Romans 5:8 suggests, God's love is the basis for Christ's death. Thus, there is no bifurcation in God between justice and mercy; wrath and love. Instead, God's wrath is the very form God's love takes in Christ's descent into hell. As Lauber interprets Barth, the descent into hell is a "divine act in which God is both the subject and the object of Jesus Christ's reconciling work."[34] This is already evident in the passage from *Credo* above and becomes fully fleshed out in the *Church Dogmatics*. With God as both subject and object, Barth avoids Calvin's error of separating the atonement from his doctrine of God, thereby turning the cross and the work of Christ into a human act alone. Lauber puts it this way:

> Christ does not suffer solely under the wrath of God (wrath of God abstracted from God's love) and in this suffering move God's disposition towards humanity

---

32. Lauber, "Hell," 93.
33. Lauber, "Hell," 93.
34. Lauber, *Barth on the Descent*, 14.

from wrath to love. Rather, God's wrath is a function of God's love. Therefore, divine love is the source for what took place on the cross, and this love is never jeopardized by the resistance and disobedience of sinful humanity. God's holy love works itself out in the destruction of sin and of human persons as sinners, and this destruction takes place in the outpouring of God's wrath upon Jesus Christ.[35]

God's justice and and mercy are not at odds with one another. God's love is unified in purpose and takes the form of wrath in order to eradicate sin and human beings as sinners as an act of kindness toward the misery of his creatures. As Lauber puts it: "Wrath is the form that divine love takes in the face of resistance and opposition."[36] In freedom, God chooses to show grace toward the creation and enter into a covenantal relationship with his creatures. It is because the cross is an act in which God is both subject and object that the integrity of God's holy love remains.

Against both Lutheran and Catholic theology, the descent for Barth (and Reformed theology) is not "a spatial journey by the exalted Jesus Christ to engage in battle with the devil and release the captive believers."[37] Barth follows Calvin in identifying the descent with the suffering of Christ on Good Friday:

> On Good Friday itself—and not only on Good Friday but "all the time He lived on earth"—the suffering of Jesus, just because it is the suffering of God's wrath against the whole human race, has no frontier, no meaning, no future. How could He who actually places Himself where

---

35. Lauber, *Barth on the Descent*, 15.

36. Lauber, *Barth on the Descent*, 17.

37. Lauber, *Barth on the Descent*, 12. As noted above, the harrowing motif is featured not only in medieval art but also literature. Christ's harrowing of hell is referenced in Dante's *Inferno*. In the *Inferno*, the pilgrim Dante questions his guide Virgil, "Did any ever leave here, through his merit or with another's help, and go to bliss?" Virgil replies, "I was a novice in this place when I saw a mighty lord descend to us who wore the sign of victory as his crown" (Dante, *Inferno*, 99). Virgil goes on to name the many Old Testament faithful who were so redeemed.

> the whole human race stands, namely, under the wrath of God—and Jesus *did* place himself there!—how could he see a frontier, a meaning, and a future in what He had there to suffer? The abyss into which sin hurls us, yes us, is just this, that we do not know how deep this abyss actually is, this suffering *without* frontiers, *without* meaning, and *without* future. This burden can only be borne. And Jesus bears it.[38]

In truth, no mere human could bear the wrath of God and the sin of the world. As Lauber succinctly puts it: "Only God can endure God's wrath without being destroyed."[39] So it is that Jesus bears it. As Barth writes in his *Doctrine of Reconciliation*: "God shows himself to be the great and true God in the fact that He can and will let His grace bear this cost, that He is capable and willing and ready for this condescension, this act of extravagance, the far journey"—the far journey that even leads Jesus into the depths of hell.[40] In this passage from *Credo*, Barth also suggests that the victory of the cross can only be understood as victory on this side of Easter. Good Friday, apart from the resurrection, is utterly dark and meaningless. Jesus's suffering is so overwhelming that even he cannot see the salvation that is accomplished in it. This comports with the Reformed tradition's insistence that the descent into hell belongs to Christ's state of humiliation (*status exaninitionis* or *humiliationis*) and not his state of exultation (*status exaltationis*).[41] The disciples, too, would have also experienced the story of salvation as it unfolded in despair and meaninglessness, without an inkling of hope left for them on Good Friday or Holy Saturday.

Nevertheless, when viewed from this side of the resurrection, it is precisely through Christ's descent that there is victory—and now, hope—for humanity. In *Church Dogmatics* 2.2, Barth picks

---

38. Barth, *Credo*, 78–79.
39. Lauber, *Barth on the Descent*, 19.
40. Barth, *CD*, 4.1:159.
41. See Lauber, *Barth on the Descent*, 12. Also see *Westminster Larger Catechism*, questions 46, 49, and 50, which reference Christ's state of humiliation.

up the theme of Christ's descent into hell in the context of his discussion on "The Determination of the Rejected." He says this:

> It is a serious matter to be threatened by hell, sentenced to hell, worthy of hell, and already on the road to hell. On the other hand, we must not minimize the fact that we actually know of only one certain triumph of hell—the handing-over of Jesus—and that this triumph of hell took place in order that it would never again be able to triumph over anyone. We must not deny that Jesus gave Himself up into the depths of hell, not only with many others but on their behalf, in their place, in the place of all who believe in Him.[42]

The descent into hell is none other than Christ's death in God-abandonment. This death is as the Rejected of God. Barth writes of Christ as the Rejected in the context of his doctrine of election and it is indeed as the Rejected that Christ is God's elected one in whom Humanity is now also elected. He writes:

> Jesus Christ is the Rejected of God, for God makes Himself rejected in Him, and has Himself alone tasted to the depths all that rejection means and necessarily involves. . . . We know of none whom God has wholly and exclusively abandoned to himself. We know only of One who was abandoned in this way, only of One who was lost. This One is Jesus Christ. And He was lost (and found again) in order that none should be lost apart from Him.[43]

Christ's suffering God-forsakenness, as the Rejected, is uniquely his own. He alone has tasted the full measure of God's wrath in the depths of hell and he does so for us.

The *pro nobis* character of the atonement is explored in *Church Dogmatics* 4.1 under the subheading "The Judge Judged in Our Place." In this section, Barth unpacks what it means for God to be both subject and object of the reconciling work of Christ.

---

42. Barth, *CD*, 2.2:496.
43. Barth, *CD*, 2.2:496.

God in Christ is both the subject, the judge, and also the object of reconciliation, the one judged in our place (or, to use the language of his doctrine of election, the Rejected). While Barth certainly affirms the substitutionary and vicarious character of the atonement (*pro nobis*), as we have seen already, he "moves beyond the static, mechanistic, and transactional character of common 'satisfaction' and 'penal substitution' theories."[44] Barth refuses to separate the person and work of Christ and instead "focuses on the narrative history of Jesus Christ—the narrated history of the unique and particular individual—the one who bears the name Jesus Christ."[45] This is a narrative of suffering, the suffering of God in Christ. Barth writes:

> We are not dealing merely with any suffering but with the suffering of God and this man in face of the destruction which threatens all creation and every individual, thus compromising God as the Creator. We are dealing with the painful confrontation of God and this man not merely with any evil, not merely with death, but with eternal death, with the power of that which is not. Therefore, we are not dealing with any sin, or with many sins, which might wound God again and again, and only especially perhaps at this point, and the consequences of which this man had only to suffer in part and freely willed to do so. We are dealing with sin itself and as such: the preoccupation, the orientation, the determination of man as he has left his place as a creature and broken his covenant with God; the corruption which God has made his own, for which He willed to take responsibility in this one man. Here, in the passion in which, as Judge, He lets Himself be judged, God has fulfilled this responsibility. In the place of all men, He has Himself wrestled with that which separates them from Him. He has Himself borne the consequences of this separation to bear it away.[46]

---

44. Lauber, *Barth on the Descent*, 3.
45. Lauber, *Barth on the Descent*, 2.
46. Barth, *CD*, 4.1:247.

In Christ, God has made the state and fate of humanity his own. God has chosen to take on not just sins but also sin itself, not just death but also eternal death. On the cross, God is both judge and judged as well as he who suffers the terrible judgment. God chooses to be this sort of God for us.

In sum, we see that, while Barth remains firmly planted in the Reformed tradition's understanding of the descent as interpretive of the suffering of the cross, he pushes beyond the errors of Calvin's transactional theology of atonement. Barth grounds the atonement in the doctrine of God. This enables him to understand the cross as a divine act, through and through, where God is both subject and object, both judge and the one judged. The judgment that Christ endures—God-abandonment, the full weight of sin, and eternal death, in short, the descent into hell—is *pro nobis*. In the end, however, Barth's theology is not a theology of Holy Saturday. His understanding of the descent into hell is focused exclusively on interpreting Christ's suffering on the cross. Even still, Barth's understanding of the descent illuminates a theology of the atonement grounded in a solid doctrine of God.

## Balthasar's Theology of Holy Saturday

Above all, it is Catholic theologian Hans Urs von Balthasar who has carved out a unique theological space for Holy Saturday. In a Holy Saturday sermon, delivered over the radio in 1956, he invites us into this space:

> What is it that takes place on Holy Saturday? What kind of day is this on which, as the old hymn says (and it is followed here by Hegel and Nietzsche), "God is dead?" The world's meaning, the purpose of existence, is dead and buried; the object of our faith, our hope and our love, is stolen from us, so that, literally, we are cast down and left alone in an unspeakable void, disappointed and forsaken: "Are you the only visitor to Jerusalem who does not know the things that have happened there in these days? . . . Concerning Jesus of Nazareth . . . we had hoped he

was the one to redeem Israel. Yes, and besides all this, it is now the third day since this happened." In between came the day of death, the day when life had no being. Not merely a day when life and its meaning faded for a while, when hope had become somewhat sleepy.... No. On this day, the world's meaning died and was buried without any hope of the resulting hiatus ever being bridged: there was no hope of ever closing the rift opened up by this death.... There is a total end and there is a total beginning, but ... what comes in between them?[47]

One suggestion of what comes in between is Christ's triumphant "harrowing of hell" and his preaching to the dead. This view, beautifully portrayed in Eastern Orthodox iconography, imagines Jesus breaking the gates of hell to overthrow the powers of evil. Balthasar rejects this motif as mythical and unfounded in Scripture. For him, it negates the reality of death as a total end. Even still, he wants to affirm the tradition of Christ's descent into hell. In his view, however, there is no action performed in Christ's descent, for Christ is truly dead. In the descent, the judgment of the cross finds its completion and end in a passive, as he calls it, "going to the dead."[48] Balthasar interprets the "being dead" of Christ as the pain of loss (*poena damni*). Christ alone experiences the full measure of separation from God.[49] It is a deep mystery how the Son of God suffers the loss of the beatific vision. Nevertheless, it is an experience of Jesus as the Son of God. Balthasar, with Barth, sees God as both subject and object in Jesus's death. It is a human death and a human going to the dead. Even so, Balthasar's thoroughly Chalcedonian Christology demands a real communication of properties (*communicatio idiomatum*) in the hypostatic union. The human suffering of Jesus is truly God's suffering. In this going

---

47. Balthasar, "We Walked," 89–90. The hymn referenced in this quote is Johann Rist's "O Darkest Woe!" Later German editions changed the line "God is dead" to negate the implied patripassianism. The English translations have followed suit and it usually reads, "God's Son is dead."

48. Balthasar, *Mysterium Paschale*, 148–49.

49. Balthasar, *Mysterium Paschale*, 168.

to the dead of Holy Saturday, Jesus suffers both the experience of sin as such and the second death. The irony of Christ's solidarity with the dead is that only he knows this experience in its terrible full measure. Balthasar writes: "If through the grace of Christ, working by anticipation, those who lived before Christ in love did not experience the entire, truly merited, *poena damni* ... who then did really experience it save the Redeemer himself? Is not precisely this inequality the final consequence of the law of solidarity?"[50] Whereas Barth identifies the descent with God-forsakenness on the cross, Balthasar suggests that it is in Christ's going to the dead that the penalty of sin and death are suffered in full measure.[51]

Balthasar poetically writes of this gap that opens in the being of God in the descent in *Heart of the World*:

> Greater still ... is the marvel that God was able to shrink to man's proportions ... that the eternal distance of love between Father and Son (eternally enclosing itself by the embrace of both in the Spirit) could gape wide as the distance between heaven and hell, from whose pit the Son groans his "I thirst," the Spirit now no longer anything but the huge, separating, and impassible chaos; that the Trinity could, in suffering's distorted image, so disfigure itself into the relationship between judge and sinner; that eternal love could don the mask of divine wrath; that the Abyss of Being could so deplete itself into an abyss of nothingness.[52]

Here, Balthasar so masterfully lays out how wide the gap between the Father and Son became in the descent and the disfigurement that occurs within the Trinity. Christ became the object of God's judgment in our place and was utterly forsaken by the Father. Yet, this moment was willingly chosen in the life of God from all eternity for our salvation. It is the love of Christ as obedient Son that has led him to this limit; it is the love of God the Father for his Son

---

50. Balthasar, *Mysterium Paschale*, 167.
51. See Balthasar, *Mysterium Paschale*, 169–70.
52. Balthasar, *Heart of the World*, 54.

that ultimately overcomes it; and it is the Spirit that is the Holy Love between them that persists—even in the abyss.

Nevertheless, for Balthasar, there is an unimaginable distance that breaks into the relationship between the Father and Son. The distance between sin and holiness is incomprehensible and yet, in the resurrection, we see that God's love is greater still. Indeed, God's wrath poured out upon Christ in hell is the very form that God's love takes for us and our salvation. So it is that even while Christ was in the farthest reaches away from heavenly glory, suffering the penalty of sin, becoming sin, and suffering death in the abyss, even then and there, the eternal love persisted in the being of God such that God himself was not torn asunder in this act of love for us.

Balthasar suggests that it is Christ himself who is the continuity between total end and total beginning.[53] He puts it pointedly: "He wanted to sink so low that, in the future, all falling would be a falling into him and every streamlet of bitterness and despair would henceforth run down into his lowermost abyss."[54] We see here that because Christ has descended into hell, no matter how far we fall, we fall into God's love for us. For those who find themselves dislocated in the hell of the far country, this is good news indeed. The solidarity of Christ with our God-forsakenness is so utter and complete that we need never experience its fullness.

## Holy Saturday and the Trinity

The story of Holy Saturday as God abandoning God begs many questions about the doctrine of the Trinity. As has been shown, it is in fact on this dark day that God chooses to reveal himself in the mystery of God suffering God. As a result, we can speak of the doctrine of the Trinity as the story of salvation and atonement. In *God as the Mystery of the World*, Eberhard Jungel puts it this way: "The doctrine of the Trinity is the dogma of soteriology in an

---

53. Balthasar, "We Walked," 91.
54. Balthasar, *Heart of the World*, 43.

absolute sense."⁵⁵ The story of Jesus's life, death, and resurrection is the Christian story of God. Indeed, it is God's story of God, the fullness of self-revelation. It is a story of God's love for humanity as revealed in the unity of Jesus's life and death. It is in this man, Jesus, that God as Father, Son, and Holy Spirit is revealed. Jungel writes:

> The Christian doctrine of the triune God is the epitome of the story of Jesus Christ because the reality of God's history with man comes to its truth in the differentiation of the one God into three persons of the Father, the Son, and the Holy Spirit. The doctrine of the Trinity basically has no other function than to make the story of God so true that it can be told in a responsible way. In the doctrine of the Trinity, God's historicity is thought as truth. In the power of this truth, God can be spoken of in a Christian way, God's being can be told as history.⁵⁶

The doctrine of the Trinity as story and history has been lost in the traditional distinction between the immanent and economic Trinity. God in Godself from eternity—the immanent Trinity—is divorced from who God has revealed himself to be in the sending of his Son and the giving of the Spirit—the economic Trinity. This distinction has led to a bifurcation in traditional concepts of God, a revealed God (*deus revelatus*) and a concealed God (*deus absconditus*). God in Godself is hidden, unknown, and unknowable. Jungel clarifies:

> It cannot be denied that the traditional doctrine of the Trinity has its weakness. . . . The danger is evoked by the traditional distinction between the immanent and economic Trinity. The immanent trinitarian doctrine understands God himself with no regard for his relationship to man; the economic trinitarian doctrine, by contrast, understands God's being in its relationship to man and his world. This distinction . . . is legitimate only when the economic doctrine of the Trinity deals with

55. Jungel, *God as the Mystery*, 344.
56. Jungel, *God as the Mystery*, 344.

God's history with man, and the immanent doctrine of the Trinity is its summarizing concept.[57]

Here is one of the great advances in theological clarity for which Barth should be credited. For Jungel, these distinctions can now only be spoken of as distinctions that illuminate rather than hide the fullness of God. With Rahner, it can be affirmed that "the economic Trinity is the immanent Trinity and the immanent Trinity is the economic Trinity."[58] The history of God in Christ is the revelation of who God is in Godself from all eternity.

God's being is revealed and defined precisely in this one, Jesus, and precisely in the hiddenness of cross and grave. It is precisely in the concealment of God on Holy Saturday and in death that God chooses to be revealed. Jungel writes:

> The deity of the living God—the divinity of his life and thus the vitality of God—is compatible in a very precise sense with the death of this human life. God's life is compatible with the death of Jesus in that it *bears* it. And by taking death on himself, he conquers it. As the victor over death, God discloses himself as God. In that the living God in his deity bears the seat of Jesus, in that he burdens the eternity of his being with the crucifixion of Jesus, he demonstrates his divine being as a *living* unity of life and death.[59]

On Holy Saturday God bears death. The Father chooses to abandon the Son and the Son willingly chooses to be abandoned in obedience. This is the dark mystery at the heart of the gospel—that God abandons God *pro nobis*. Balthasar is right to emphasize the passivity of the descent into hell. The descent into hell is silence, darkness, and curse. He borrows Francis of Assisi's phrase to say that it is the "obedience of a corpse,"[60] a solidarity with the dead.[61]

---

57. Jungel, *God as the Mystery*, 346.
58. Rahner, *The Trinity*, 38.
59. Jungel, *God as the Mystery*, 343–44.
60. Balthasar, *Mysterium Paschale*, 174.
61. Balthasar, *Mysterium Paschale*, 167.

Or, as Jungel puts it, "If being dead is the precise opposite of an event, then what we are saying is that, in this death, God himself was the event which happened."[62] In this death, this non-event is, at the same time, the event of God's revelation of love. In the resurrection, we see that the overflow of God's love is more powerful than death and that, indeed, this dark mystery is the fullness of its revelation. Jungel writes:

> The Kerygma of the Resurrected One proclaims the Crucified One as the self-definition of God. Only when the truth of this assertion is affirmed is it at all meaningful to speak of the Resurrected One. . . . Jesus's resurrection is not an "intervention" of God into the world's structures, which then leaves behind a new fact within this world, but does not affect the being of God. In the resurrection of Jesus, the issue is not only one of a divine action, but of the divine being itself.[63]

God's eternal being is both chosen and revealed in this act. In freedom, God from eternity has chosen to be just this God *for us*. As Barth puts it in *Church Dogmatics* 2.2:

> Predestination means that from all eternity God has determined upon man's acquittal at His own cost. It means that God has ordained that in the place of the one acquitted He Himself should be perishing and abandoned and rejected—the Lamb slain from the foundation of the world. There is, then, no background, no *decretum absolutum*, no mystery of the divine good-pleasure, in which predestination might just as well be man's rejection.[64]

The being of God revealed in this act is God in Godself from all eternity. God is love in Godself and that even in bearing sin, death, and curse, God is not destroyed or overcome in his solidarity with our "state and fate." In other words, "Death is not turned around apart from love, because love alone is able to involve itself in the

---

62. Jungel, *God as the Mystery*, 363.
63. Jungel, *God as the Mystery*, 364.
64. Barth, *CD*, 2.2:167.

complete harshness of death. In the death of Jesus, love itself was at work and revealed God as the one who is love."[65]

Rightly telling the story of Holy Saturday brings together the doctrines of the Trinity and the atonement in ways that clarify and solidify them both. While neither Barth nor Jungel speak of Holy Saturday in any direct way, they both help to provide a firm foundation for what it might mean to say that God in Christ has in fact descended into hell. With Calvin, Barth locates the fullness of the descent on the cross. Balthasar locates the fullness of Christ's descent into hell on Saturday. To speak of the descent into hell is to speak first and foremost about death. Reflection on Christ's "going to the dead" rightly finds its full end on Saturday, the day of God's silence or, dare we even say it, the day of the death of God. To understand what it might mean to speak the unspeakable about God at the very end and limit of possibility is to take seriously the complete end that occurs on the cross. Only when this death is seen as death can the story of the resurrection give hope and meaning as a new and now "possible impossibility."[66] Of course, it is only because of the resurrection that the events of cross and grave can now be known as the fullness of God's self-revelation in Christ. God abandons God and Father abandons Son, "for us and for our salvation."[67] It is only in the abiding communion of God's self-relatedness—the Spirit, the Love between Father and Son—that death and hell are taken into God's being and overcome once for all. It is in the heart of the tomb that the heart of God is fully revealed, a love revealed in and through death, a love that overcomes it. It is through the bearing of our sin, our curse, our death, our hell, and, finally, the bearing it away that new life comes.

65. Jungel, *God as the Mystery*, 363.

66. This is the language Alan Lewis applies to the mystery of Holy Saturday in his masterful outlining of a theology of Holy Saturday in Lewis, *Between Cross and Resurrection*.

67. The *pro nobis* can only be confession. Jungel says, "It is not obvious in looking at the cross of Jesus that he became a curse *for us*. The words 'for us' are a *confession*. In order to be able to add 'for us' to 'curse,' the cross must already be interpreted as the cross of Christ, the cross of the Son of God" (Jungel, *God as the Mystery*, 361).

It is in bearing hell, forsakenness, and hopelessness that the love of God overflows the bounds of the grave with Christ's resurrection and the outpouring of God's Spirit upon the church as Christ's body in the world.

## The Descent into Hell in Scripture

As noted at the outset of this chapter, Wayne Grudem vehemently opposes a biblical basis for the descent into hell. After examining the texts used for scriptural warrant, he concludes, "It is at best confusing and in most cases misleading for modern Christians. My own judgment is that there would be all gain and no loss if it were dropped from the Creed once for all."[68] The Scriptures that Grudem addresses are those typically used to support the descent into hell (Acts 2:27, Rom 10:6–7, Eph 4:8–9, 1 Pet 3:18–20, and 1 Pet 4:6). Of course, neither Barth nor Balthasar ground their theology of Christ's descent into hell in a particular text or even a set of proof texts. Barth explicitly rejects any reading of the descent into hell from these passages. He grounds it, with Calvin, firmly in the cry of dereliction—as an interpretation of Christ's experience of God abandonment.[69] In *Mysterium Paschale*, Balthasar begins his study of Holy Saturday with an examination of the biblical data. He, too, finds the received tradition of interpretation wanting, especially with regard to the mythical elements surrounding the harrowing. Even so, he sees in Scripture a basis for the several claims he makes about Christ's solidarity in death, his being dead, and the salvific character of such a death.[70] The limits of this study press against undertaking a similar such analysis. But I do I want to examine Psalm 88 as an interesting test case for the scriptural warrant for a theology of Holy Saturday.

68. Grudem, "He Did Not," 113. See also Grudem, *Systematic Theology*, 586–94.

69. See Lauber's summary of Barth's engagement with these texts in Lauber, *Barth on the Descent*, 77–80.

70. For Balthasar's examination of the scriptural warrant for Jesus's descent see Balthasar, *Mysterium Paschale*, 149–68.

First and foremost, it is important to remember that the Psalms are prayers addressed to God. Indeed, the book of Psalms is often referred to as the "prayerbook of the Bible." Throughout Psalms, we encounter the range of human experience and emotion, but it is always in the context of the praise and worship of God. With an address to God comes the assumption that God hears and acts. Psalm 88 is no different in this regard. Beginning with verse 1, the entire psalm is addressed to God—and not just any God, but the God of Israel, Yahweh. Old Testament scholar Walter Brueggemann suggests that these lamentations only make sense "when the premise of the credo holds."[71] In other words, the only possible reason for such an address is that it is grounded in a faith that God does act on behalf of God's people. This is part of the unique witness of the Church. We do not simply protest against suffering (although we do) but, more than that, we also bring our lamentations before God in prayer with faith in God's activity as a community and individual believers.

Lament, Brueggemann argues, is speech of disorientation. Lament pours forth from believers who are experiencing life on the edge. The old order of life has proven unreliable and chaos has ensued.[72] This most certainly includes life on the other side of the trauma of war. There are other psalms of lament, but Psalm 88 is unique in that, much like Holy Saturday, there is no restoration, no grand reversal, and no obvious hope. One commentator suggests it is "the story of Job, half told."[73] Brueggemann purports, "The angriest, most hopeless [of lament psalms] is Psalm 88, which ends in unreserved, unrelieved gloom."[74] For Brueggemann, Psalm 88 does not just take us to the edge of this pit of disorientation, he describes it as a "full descent" into its depths.[75] From the bottom of this pit there is no clear way out. He writes:

71. Brueggemann, *Abiding Astonishment*, 52.
72. Brueggemann, *Praying the Psalms*, 18.
73. Wellhausen, citation unknown.
74. Brueggemann, *Praying the Psalms*, 18.
75. Brueggemann, *Message of the Psalms*, 77.

> Faith does not always resolve life. There is not for every personal crisis of disorientation a way out, if only we press the right button. Too much pastoral action is inclined and tempted to resolve things, no matter how the situation really is. Faith is treated like the great answer book. Insofar as these psalms are witnesses to faith, they attest that faith means staying in the midst of the disorientation, not retreating to an old orientation that is over and done with, and not charging ahead to some imagined resolution that rushes ahead of the slow tortuous pace of reality.[76]

As Brueggemann suggests, "faith does not always resolve life."[77] Psalm 88 poignantly illustrates this for us. The Psalmist can no longer imagine any possibility beyond death and the grave. The question, then, becomes: how do we live in the disorientation, even when death is all we can perceive? What is our Christian witness when life goes to hell? This terror is not unknown to the psalmist who lays his suffering squarely at God's feet: "Your wrath has spread over me; your dread assaults destroy me" (Ps 88:16). He can bring this protest to God precisely because of his faith in God's justice. The psalmist's faith in God is grounded in an understanding of reality that transcends his immediate experience. Just as it would be wrong to pull this psalm out of the context of the psalmist's Jewish faith, likewise, it would be wrong for us to pull Psalm 88 out of the context of the book of Psalms as a whole or the entirety of Scripture. It is the same God we find at creation, in the Exodus event, and in Jesus Christ that is addressed here. I say that not as a way of making an end run around the disorientation; rather, as a way for us to find our way through it. What, then, is our Christian witness when life goes to hell?

Though often criticized by modern scholars, I think the early Church Fathers were on fairly good footing to read Scripture Christologically. Chrysostom, Ambrose, and Cyril of Jerusalem all

---

76. Brueggemann, *Message of the Psalms*, 78.
77. Brueggemann, *Message of the Psalms*, 78.

interpret this psalm in light of Christ.[78] Our faith in God's activity is grounded in the person and work of Jesus Christ as the fullness of God's self-revelation. Therefore, with the help of Dietrich Bonhoeffer, I would like to offer up that we might do the same. We find such help in the last book Bonhoeffer published before his imprisonment—a very short volume on the Psalms called *The Prayerbook of the Bible*. In it, he suggests this:

> In Jesus's mouth, the human word becomes God's Word. When we pray along with the prayer of Christ, God's word becomes again a human word. Thus, all prayers of the Bible are such prayers, which we pray together with Jesus Christ, prayers in which Christ includes us, and through which Christ brings us before the face of God. Otherwise there are no true prayers, for only in and with Jesus Christ can we truly pray.
>
> If we want to read and to pray the prayers of the Bible, and especially the Psalms, we must not, therefore, first ask what they have to do with us, but what they have to do with Jesus Christ.... Thus, it does not matter whether the Psalms express exactly what we feel in our heart at the moment we pray. Perhaps it is precisely the case that we must pray against our own heart in order to pray rightly.[79]

Bonhoeffer's suggestion is that when we pray the Psalms, we join Christ in prayer. Indeed, all our prayer is prayed with and through Christ. The Psalms are not simply the cries of the human heart to God. How, then, could they be the Word of God for us in Scripture? They are the prayers of God to God. As part of the body of Christ, we are called to join in praying these prayers through Christ. When we pray Psalm 88, we are not simply addressing God, we are addressing God our Father with Christ. He alone has experienced the fullness of God's silence and abandonment in the

---

78. See Chrysostom, *Demonstration against the Pagans* 4.12; Ambrose, *Letter 59*; Cyril of Jerusalem, *Catechetical Lectures* 14.8.

79. Bonhoeffer, *Prayerbook*, 157.

grave. He willingly suffered the weight of our sin and God's wrath. What is our Christian witness when life goes to hell? The Psalmist's cry for help is precisely that the grave is outside the bounds of salvation. Yet, Jesus Christ himself has gone into the depths of hell for us. When we pray, we can be assured that God's "steadfast love *is* declared in the grave" (Ps 88:11). God has gone into this pit of disorientation ahead of us, even into the very pit of hell, that God might be with us there. To pray this psalm with Christ is to catch a glimpse of his cry of dereliction on the cross: "My God, my God, why have you forsaken me?" (Matt 27:46). The despair and rejection that we read of in Psalm 88 are in fact the very form of God's love for us.[80] God has joined in solidarity even with our God-abandonment (Rom 8:39).

## Conclusion

The story of Holy Saturday has been traced through the creedal confession of Christ's descent into hell. Starting with Calvin and tracing through Barth, the descent into hell was seen to be foundational to a full understanding of the atonement. Barth provided helpful theological correctives to Calvin's doctrine by grounding the atonement in the doctrine of God. Balthasar provided a challenge to consider that the fullness of God-abandonment Christ suffers continues in the grave through a passive "going to the dead." With Jungel, it was seen that in the crucified one, the dead Jesus, God reveals himself most fully. The doctrine of the Trinity and soteriology are seen in sharpest relief against the backdrop of Holy Saturday.

In the end, it has been shown that the suffering of God in Christ on Holy Saturday provides a place from which to think theologically about and, ultimately, to minister pastorally to those who suffer. A theology of Holy Saturday takes seriously the sin

---

80. I think it is fitting that this psalm should find its place in worship on Holy Saturday, although it is nowhere to be found in the Revised Common Lectionary. On this day of all days, the dark depths of God's love for us should be read from Holy Scripture.

and death we suffer in our humanity. On this day, "between cross and resurrection," we find the place of death and hopelessness in the very life of God. Yet, in light of the resurrection, it is seen that it is precisely in the silence of Holy Saturday and the mystery of Christ's descent into hell that all hope is born. The fullness of God's love is revealed in the hiddenness of this day and God's presence is revealed precisely in God's absence. This is good news for those stuck in the far country.

*3*

# A Chalcedonian Conception of Trauma and Moral Injury[1]

IN CARING FOR VETERANS, pastoral caregivers need to have an understanding of the symptoms of PTSD they may encounter in the stories soldiers tell them as well as a basic grasp of the important features of moral injury.[2] A working knowledge of these clinical diagnoses and their symptoms is useful in order to educate or refer veterans to the appropriate helping resources or to collaborate with interdisciplinary colleagues. Nevertheless, clinical diagnosis and treatment of PTSD or moral injury are not the business of the pastoral caregiver. In *Spiritual Care*, Dietrich Bonhoeffer writes:

> The goal of spiritual care should never be a change of mental condition.... I do not provide *decisive* help for anyone if I turn a sad person into a cheerful one, a timid person into a courageous one. That would be a secular—and not a real—help. Beyond and within circumstances such as sadness and timidity it should be believed that God is our help and comfort. Christ and his victory over health and sickness, luck and misfortune, birth and

---

1. This chapter was also published in *Pro Ecclesia* as Tietje, "Contra."
2. For symptoms and clinical diagnosis criteria of PTSD, see *DSM-V*, 271–80.

death must be proclaimed. The help he brings is forgiveness and new life out of death.³

Or, as Karl Barth writes about the cure of souls (an ancient term for pastoral care):

> Seldom or never will this [cure of souls] occur without the unconscious—and why not the conscious?—presupposition and sometimes application of various forms of general or secular and therefore neutral psychology, psychogogics, and psychotherapy. This does not alter the fact, however, that the problems of the cure of souls begin where those of a neutral psychology and the neutral art of healing based upon it cease. It can thus understand the problems of the latter and include them in its own discussions, but it cannot take them over or try to solve them.⁴

The goal of pastoral care is distinct from psychotherapy. The goal of psychotherapy is, as Bonhoeffer puts it, a "change of mental condition."⁵ The pastoral caregiver's concern is for the soul, defined by Barth as "the totality of a human being in his individual personal existence" in relation to God.⁶ As Eduard Thurneysen writes: "When we inquire about a man's soul in the context of pastoral care, we are concerned neither with scientific anthropology (whether biological or psychological) nor with philosophical anthropology (whether materialistic or idealistic) . . . our inquiry is a purely theological one."⁷

In order to properly relate the concerns of the pastoral caregiver and the psychotherapist for the soldier who experiences PTSD or moral injury, it is necessary to first step back and consider the relationship between the fields of theology and psychology, generally. As Barth suggests, the cure of souls will unlikely

---

3. Bonhoeffer, *Spiritual Care*, 30.
4. Barth, *CD*, 4.3.2:886.
5. Bonhoeffer, *Spiritual Care*, 30.
6. Barth, *CD*, 4.3.2:885.
7. Thurneysen, *Pastoral Care*, 54.

take place without the presupposition or application, consciously or unconsciously, of some sort of psychology. Even so, as he says, "The problems of the cure of souls begin where those of a neutral psychology and the neutral art of healing based upon it cease."[8] The problems of psychology may be framed and understood from a theological perspective, but, according to Barth, it is not the task of theology to try to solve them. Much is implicit here in Barth's conception of the relationship between theology and psychology that needs to be fleshed out.

In her book, *Theology and Pastoral Counseling: A New Interdisciplinary Approach,* Deborah Hunsinger expounds a truly Barthian conception of the relationship between the disciplines of theology and psychology by applying Barth's "Chalcedonian pattern" to the two disciplines. Hunsinger notes that, "Since the defining terms of the pattern, as Barth uses it, are formal rather than material, they can be applied to a wide range of doctrinal or substantive questions."[9] It will be seen that employing the Chalcedonian pattern to relate theology and psychology will be useful for both constructive and critical purposes. In what follows, I outline the Chalcedonian pattern as it applies to the disciplines of theology and psychology. Next, I apply the pattern to Shelly Rambo's work, which uses trauma as a lens through which to construct a theology of Holy Saturday—or, as she calls it, "a theology of remaining." I suggest that the theological shortcomings of her work are a direct result of her flawed methodology. Rambo's " theology of remaining" fails to account for the logical priority of theological claims as well as the asymmetry of the theological and the psychological discourse. Consequently, she jettisons the Trinitarian underpinnings of Hans Urs von Balthasar's theology of Holy Saturday. The Chalcedonian pattern, I conclude, is needed to make a clear distinction between the psychological conceptions of trauma and moral injury and a pastoral theological understanding of trauma and moral injury as soul wounds.

8. Barth, *CD*, 4.3.2:886.
9. Deborah Hunsinger, *Pastoral Counseling*, 61.

## The Chalcedonian Pattern

In 451 CE, the Council of Chalcedon was called to address Monophysitism, the belief that Christ has one nature (*monos+physis*=one nature). Monophysites upheld the divine nature of Christ at the expense of his full humanity. In response, the Council of Chalcedon produced a *Definition of Faith* that affirmed the *Nicene Creed* of 325 CE and its clarification at Constantinople in 381 CE.[10] The Council's *Definition of Faith* affirmed both Christ's full divinity and humanity as existing "in two natures which undergo no confusion, no change, no division, no separation; at no point was the difference between the natures taken away through the union, but rather the property of both natures is preserved and comes together into a single person and a single subsistent being."[11] This definition suggests that while Jesus's divine and human natures remain distinct (without confusion or change), they cannot be separated. They are an integral unity in the person of Jesus Christ (without separation or division). In addition to distinction and inseparability, the third aspect of the Chalcedonian pattern rests on Barth's understanding of what it means to say that the "property of both natures is preserved."[12] Deborah Hunsinger suggests that, "According to Barth's interpretation of Chalcedon, Jesus's divine and human natures, each present in a complete or unabridged way, were to be understood not only as related without separation or division and without confusion or change but also with conceptual priority assigned to the divine over the human nature."[13] This ordering of the relationship between Christ's humanity and divinity is of the utmost importance when it comes to understanding the events of cross and grave. In the divine-human union, it is the priority of Christ's divinity that renders his suffering and death as salvific for us.[14] Yet, even with the priority of Christ's divinity, his

---

10. Pelikan and Hotchkiss, *Creeds and Confessions*, 1:172–73.
11. Pelikan and Hotchkiss, *Creeds and Confessions*, 1:172–73.
12. Pelikan and Hotchkiss, *Creeds and Confessions*, 1:173.
13. Hunsinger, *Pastoral Counseling*, 62.
14. In chapter 2, divine priority was outlined in the guise of Barth's

humanity is not overshadowed or rendered superfluous. This conceptual ordering does not destroy the integrity of Jesus's humanity.

This ordering is not a hierarchical relationship wherein the difference between divinity and humanity would be one of degree. According to George Hunsinger, "The two natures are rather conceived as asymmetrically related, for they share no common measure or standard of measurement.... Although there is a divine priority and a human subsequence, their asymmetry allows a conception which avoids hierarchical domination in favor of *a mutual ordering in freedom*."[15] This asymmetrical relationship between divinity and humanity is fundamental for understanding the relationship between theology and psychology. The subjects of the two disciplines are not materially equivalent and share no common measure or standard.

Barth's vivid Chalcedonian imagination is seen to be operative in several other contexts, one being the relationship between body and soul. Body and soul are undeniably different, and yet they cannot be separated from one another. As Hunsinger points out, a person is:

> An "embodied soul" and a "besouled body."... Yet, in the conceptual ordering of this differentiated unity, the soul is first and the body is second.... A human being is the soul of his or her body as established by God. He or she is (and here is the Chalcedonian pattern) "soul and body totally and simultaneously, in indissoluble differentiation, inseparable unity and indestructible order."[16]

Deborah Hunsinger also highlights how, in Barth, the human responses of gratitude, obedience, and faith are dependent on and logically subsequent to God's prior action of grace, command, and promise. Grace and gratitude, command and obedience, and promise and faith occur in a single event wherein God and

---

understanding of God as both subject and object on Good Friday and Holy Saturday.

15. George Hunsinger, *Karl Barth*, 286–87.
16. Hunsinger, *Pastoral Counseling*, 64.

humanity each retain their freedom and integrity. God's gracious action does not manipulate or coerce and yet, free human response is entirely dependent upon it and subsequent to it.[17] Here, the three features of the Chalcedonian pattern are seen as well: "Indissoluble differentiation, inseparable unity, and indestructible order."[18]

This pattern can also be seen to inform Barth's interpretation of the healing of the paralytic in Mark 2.

> When Jesus saw their faith, he said to the paralytic, "Son, your sins are forgiven." Now some of the scribes were sitting there, questioning in their hearts, "Why does this fellow speak in this way? It is blasphemy! Who can forgive sins but God alone?" At once, Jesus perceived in his spirit that they were discussing these questions among themselves; and he said to them, "Why do you raise such questions in your hearts? Which is easier, to say to the paralytic, 'Your sins are forgiven,' or to say, 'Stand up and take your mat and walk'? But so that you may know that the Son of Man has authority on earth to forgive sins"—he said to the paralytic—"I say to you, stand up, take your mat, and go to your home." And he stood up, and immediately took the mat, and went out before all of them; so that they were all amazed and glorified God, saying, "We have never seen anything like this!" (Mark 2:5–12)

Barth looks at this parable and the relationship between healing and forgiveness through the lens of "sign" and "thing signified." Barth writes:

> We can separate form and content, sign and thing signified. But we cannot derive them from each other, any more than we can separate them from each other, by any method of calculation. . . . The forgiveness of sins is manifestly the thing signified, while the healing is the sign, quite inseparable from, but very significantly

---

17. Hunsinger, *Pastoral Counseling*, 65.
18. Barth, *CD*, 3.2:437.

## A Chalcedonian Conception of Trauma

related to, this thing signified, yet neither identical with it nor a condition of it: "That ye may know."[19]

We see here all three aspects of the Chalcedonian pattern at work. There is most certainly an indissoluble differentiation between the healing and the forgiveness of sins in this narrative. There is also an inseparable unity in this one act. Significantly, there is also an asymmetrical relationship between forgiveness and healing (indestructible order). The healing is a sign that is logically subsequent and dependent upon the forgiveness. It occurs "that you may know." Forgiveness, however, does not, in turn, point to or signify healing in the same way. It is the free, gracious act of God in Christ in no way dependent upon the healing. Healing, in general, can still be seen as independent of salvation. Workers in healing professions work toward healing with no need for an account of salvation. Yet, from a theological perspective, we can see that all healing is so ordered as to point as a sign toward salvation (forgiveness).

This logical ordering of priority (of forgiveness) and subsequence (of healing) is seen as a matter of "priority in definition." Philosopher W. F. R. Hardie says, "*A* is logically prior to *B* when the definition of *B* mentions *A*, but the definition of *A* does not mention *B*."[20] For Barth, it would certainly be the case that the definition of forgiveness would be quite independent of healing and that healing would most certainly be defined in reference to its role as a sign of forgiveness. This is because, as Hunsinger writes: "The kind of definitional or logical priority that we are speaking of, therefore, clearly has to do with the arrangement of therapeutic concepts in relation to theological beliefs."[21] In other words, to speak of the ordering of the relationship between healing and forgiveness brings us very near the task of relating psychology and theology using the Chalcedonian pattern.

19. Barth, *CD*, 1.2:189.
20. Hardie, *Aristotle's Ethical Theory*, 52, quoted in Hunsinger, *Pastoral Counseling*, 67.
21. Hunsinger, *Pastoral Counseling*, 67.

The indissoluble differentiation between forgiveness and healing is grounded in their conceptual independence. The formal logic for conceptual independence can be outlined as follows:

> A conceptual account of $X$ is an account of what we mean, understand, and intend ourselves to be talking about, when we talk or think about $X$. If $X$ is not correctly thus accounted for in terms of $Y$, then $X$ is conceptually independent of $Y$.[22]

The theological concept of forgiveness can be seen as conceptually independent from any psychological conception of healing and vice versa. Deborah Hunsinger thinks this definition of conceptual independence draws near to what it might mean to relate theology and psychology in a Barthian way, that is, according to the Chalcedonian pattern.[23]

Theology and psychology are two different conceptual and language worlds. These differences should not be denied or made ambiguous. If the concepts of salvation and healing are brought in relation to one another, as in the story of the healing of the paralytic, then it is healing that is accounted for in terms of salvation ("that you may know"). The theological concept of salvation is logically prior to and conceptually independent of any psychological or biological conception of healing. Salvation and forgiveness are a function of God's relationship with humanity and thus are concepts of an entirely different order than the concepts of psychology. Certainly, the concept of healing has a relative conceptual independence. It is possible to speak of a healing apart from salvation. In Luke 17, Jesus heals ten lepers, but only one returns and finds salvation. This story illustrates a clear distinction between healing and salvation. However, from a Barthian theological perspective, ultimately, healing of body and mind remains dependent upon and is a sign of salvation. Hunsinger sums up the relationship this way: "Although psychological categories are both logically independent of *and* dependent on theological categories in different

22. Hurley, *Natural Reasons*, 10, quoted in Hunsinger, *Karl Barth*, 287.
23. Hunsinger, *Pastoral Counseling*, 68.

ways, theological categories are by definition both logically prior to and independent of psychological categories with respect to their significance."[24]

Hunsinger cautions that the Chalcedonian pattern is useful for clarifying the relationship of theological and psychological concepts. Much like the healing and forgiveness of the paralytic, theological and psychological realities are inseparable *in reality*. Any event may be examined conceptually from the perspective of theology or psychology, and yet, *in reality*, these aspects cannot be separated.[25] With this in mind, it can be seen that the three aspects of the Chalcedonian pattern (indissoluble differentiation, inseparable unity, and indestructible order) are useful for both critical and constructive purposes when examining the relationship between the fields of psychology and theology.

## A Chalcedonian Critique of Rambo's "Theology of Remaining"

One promising partner in the task of speaking theologically in the aftermath of trauma is the work of Shelly Rambo in *Spirit and Trauma: A Theology of Remaining*. Rambo wrestles theologically with the struggles of New Orleans pastors in the aftermath of Hurricane Katrina. One such pastor, Deacon Julius Lee, concludes that, "The storm is gone, but the 'after the storm' is always here."[26] For Rambo, this experience of the "after" is the quintessential experience of trauma. She writes: "Studies in trauma suggest that trauma has a double structure: the actual occurrence of a violent event(s) and a belated awakening to the event. Trauma is not solely located in the actual event but, instead, encompasses the return of that event, the ways in which the event is not concluded."[27] As was seen in chapter 1, this falls very much in line with the neurobiological ways

24. Hunsinger, *Pastoral Counseling*, 69.
25. Hunsinger, *Pastoral Counseling*, 69.
26. Rambo, *Spirit and Trauma*, 1.
27. Rambo, *Spirit and Trauma*, 7.

in which PTSD is grounded in the re-experiencing of a traumatic event that has not been integrated as a memory of the past. The overwhelming force of the event has left it lingering intrusively as a present experience. If trauma is an encounter with death, it is an encounter that persists. In light of the persistence of past trauma as present reality—this "after" quality—Rambo suggests that trauma opens up the "middle," a "perplexing space of survival."[28] It is a place where "death and life are no longer bounded."[29] It is this middle space that Rambo seeks to explore theologically. She writes:

> The good news of Christianity for those who experience trauma rests in the capacity to theologize this middle. It does not rest in either the event of cross or resurrection, but instead in the movement between the two—movements that I identify through the concept of witness. The good news lies in the ability of Christian theology to witness between death and life, in its ability to forge a new discourse between the two.[30]

To do this, Rambo takes trauma to be the interpretive lens through which to read the Christian story and, in turn, do theology.

This hermeneutics of trauma is at the center of Rambo's work. She suggests that:

> The insights of trauma actually constitute the hermeneutical lens through which an alternative vision of healing and redemption emerges.... Trauma is the key to articulating a theology of redemption rather than the problem around which theology must navigate. The dynamics of trauma guide my readings and I refer to them as the 'lens of trauma' through which theological claims about healing and redemption must be newly forged.[31]

Rambo contends that the lens of trauma is not simply the importation of the insights of trauma theory into theology. She writes:

28. Rambo, *Spirit and Trauma*, 7.
29. Rambo, *Spirit and Trauma*, 7.
30. Rambo, *Spirit and Trauma*, 8.
31. Rambo, *Spirit and Trauma*, 11.

"The relationship between theology and trauma theory does not rest in the degree to which theologians employ insights from trauma into the discipline of theology but in a resonance between the two languages."[32] She goes on: "Theology hears itself differently in the language of trauma. . . . This witness from within a discourse [theology] is made possible through another [trauma theory], but this meeting point is the site of trauma."[33] Trauma itself is the lens, and not trauma theory, through which she seeks to read the Christian story. "Trauma theory," according to Rambo, "like deconstruction, is a way of reading that exposes the gaps and fissures in the texts."[34] Unfortunately, there is no lens of trauma in and of itself, apart from the interpretation she gives it in light of trauma theory. As a result, she reads both the Gospel of John and Hans Urs von Balthasar's theology of Holy Saturday through the lens of trauma theory's deconstructionist methodology. Like trauma theorists, she probes these texts for the gaps and fissures in an "attempt to give expression to what cannot be fully known."[35]

It is through the lens of trauma or, perhaps more properly, trauma theory, that Rambo comes to explore the middle space of Holy Saturday.[36] It is here that she finds the day "after" the trauma of Good Friday untouched by the resurrection of Easter Sunday. It is after a complete end and without a new beginning. It is here that she finds the theological mirror image to the middle space of trauma, between knowing and unknowing, between life and death. What her probing of gaps and fissures amounts to, unfortunately, is creative fiction when it comes to reading her sources. Most

32. Rambo, *Spirit and Trauma*, 31.
33. Rambo, *Spirit and Trauma*, 31–32.
34. Rambo, *Spirit and Trauma*, 31.
35. Rambo, *Spirit and Trauma*, 31.
36. I owe a debt of gratitude to Rambo for suggesting Holy Saturday as a conceptual space for thinking theologically about trauma and for the introduction of Balthasar's work as a starting point to do so. Hers was the first book I read when I redeployed from Afghanistan and she graciously responded to some questions I asked while still deployed. While I disagree with both her methodology and conclusions, her work remains an important contribution to the discussion about trauma and a theology of Holy Saturday.

significantly, she refuses to accept Balthasar's very orthodox (and Augustinian) Trinitarian presentation of the Spirit as the bond of love between the loving Father and the beloved Son. She writes:

> Balthasar presents the Spirit in a form consistent with Trinitarian orthodoxy. This securing Spirit ensures that the Godhead does not sever, that the divine Being can die but not die a tragic death. In a sense, the Spirit *is* the necessary hinge between tragedy and triumph.... Spirit is the secure bridge that keeps this love story from being a tragic one. But could Spirit, drawing on images from *Heart of the World*, be the weary love that forges a path through the pathless dark of hell?[37]

The passage in Balthasar's *Heart of the World* to which she refers is this one:

> The magic of Holy Saturday. The chaotic fountain remains directionless. Could this be the residue of the Son's love which, poured out to the last when every vessel cracked and the old world perished, is now making a path for itself to the Father through the glooms of naught? Or, in spite of it all, is this love trickling on in impotence, unconsciously, laboriously, towards a new creation that does not yet even exist, a creation which is still to be lifted up and given shape?[38]

Rambo suggests: "Balthasar provides a vocabulary for Spirit here that expands beyond his stated pneumatology in the descent to hell. Between death and life, there is a testimony to Spirit, to a love that survives and remains not in victory but in weariness."[39] The problem with Rambo's reading is that this vocabulary for Spirit is something she admits is alien to Balthasar's own theology.

Indeed, the "chaotic fountain" and "residue of the Son's love" are the wound in Christ's side from which water and blood flow. What follows in the *Heart of the World* passage is rich with

---

37. Rambo, *Spirit and Trauma*, 71–72.
38. Balthasar, *Heart of the World*, 152.
39. Rambo, *Spirit and Trauma*, 80.

eucharistic imagery and comports with Balthasar's reckoning of Holy Saturday as a passive suffering. The passage continues:

> What is poured out here is no longer a present suffering, but a suffering that has been concluded—no longer now a sacrificing love, but a love sacrificed. Only the wound is there: gaping, the great open gate, the chaos, the nothingness out of which the wellspring leaps forth. Never again will this gate be shut. Just as the first creation arose ever anew out of sheer nothingness, so too, this second world—still unborn, still caught up in its first rising—will have its sole origin in this wound.... Deep-dug Fountain of Life! Wave upon wave gushes out of you inexhaustible, ever-flowing, billows of water and blood baptizing the heathen hearts, comforting the yearning souls, rushing over the deserts of guilt, enriching overabundantly, overflowing every heart that receives it, far surpassing every desire.[40]

What begins as a "chaotic fountain" becomes the "Fountain of Life." What begins as a "residue ... trickling on in impotence" becomes wave upon wave of Christ's life-giving presence in the sacraments of baptism and communion. The witness to a weary Spirit of love that Rambo posits is completely divorced from the central figure of *Heart of the World*—Jesus himself—who Balthasar imagines in this work of poetic theology as *the* heart of the world, indeed the victorious heart of the world.[41] This victory for Balthasar is no triumphalism. It is a victory precisely in death and in descent into the abyss. There is no survival of love in the abyss. Balthasar, addressing the dead Christ, writes:

> To suffer one ought to know how to love. But you no longer love: your love, which once pealed solemnly like a massive bell, now clatters as pitiably as a rattle on Good Friday. It would be too easy to suffer if one could still love. Love has been taken from you. The only thing you

---

40. Balthasar, *Heart of the World*, 152–53.

41. The entire third part of *Heart of the World* is entitled, "The Victory." See Balthasar, *Heart of the World*, 155.

> still feel is the burning void, the hollow which it has left behind. It would be a joy for you if, from the depths of hell, you could still, and for all eternity, love the Father who rejected you. But love has been taken from you. You wanted to give everything away, didn't you? It requires no great skill to give everything up so long as one can still keep love. It only gets serious when love gives itself up. Love was your Heart's heart, your soul's bread, the eternal breath of your person. You lived on love; you had no other thought but love; you were love. Now it has been taken away: you are smothering, starving; you are a stranger to yourself. You are dying the true *Liebestod*, the true love-death, for we hear love's death rattle and witness its last contortions.[42]

Indeed, Christ's descent into hell is the death of love. Rambo knows she is going beyond Balthasar's "stated pneumatology" and into decidedly un-Christologically grounded territory. To understand how she gets there, it is useful to consider her methodology in light of Hunsinger's explication of the Chalcedonian pattern of thought employed by Barth.

When the Chalcedonian pattern is applied to Rambo's work, it should be clear that to use trauma or trauma theory as a hermeneutical lens for doing theology puts trauma in the place of logical priority and conceptual independence over against theology. There is an asymmetrical relationship between theology and trauma, but in the wrong direction. It would have been interesting to see, if she had been more thoroughly Tillichian, how she might have used the method of correlation to allow the language of theology to inform and interpret trauma theory as well.[43] Of course, such a symmetrical relationship would still fall short of a proper ordering provided by the Chalcedonian pattern as Barth would understand it. The lens of trauma only allows her to see the survival and persistence of a middle space of death in life. In the end, her interpretive framework means that she fails to read both

---

42. Balthasar, *Heart of the World*, 115–16.
43. Tillich, *Systematic Theology*, 1:59–66.

## A Chalcedonian Conception of Trauma

Balthasar and Scripture on their own terms. The lens of trauma becomes another "hermeneutic of suspicion" that fails to take seriously the claims of the biblical text as it is presented.

To illustrate, Rambo suggests that Balthasar's assertion of an Augustinian Spirit that holds the Father and Son together in hell is only a matter of appeasing his critics. She goes on to imagine a pneumatology completely disconnected from both Balthasar's own work and the Augustinian Trinitarian tradition.[44] She believes that Balthasar's conformity to the tradition rescues God from the abyss. Her work would have Christ remain in the abyss, in hell. She writes: "Perhaps the divine story is neither a tragic one nor a triumphant one but, in fact, a story of divine remaining, the story of love that survives. It is a cry arising from the abyss."[45] It seems that this remaining in the abyss and this shift where "the crucified God is now the remaining God, figured in the Spirit," while certainly not triumphant, is tragic at best.[46] Balthasar recognizes that God in Christ both suffers for and with us in the descent into hell. For Rambo, by contrast, God's descent into the abyss is not in order to take upon himself our sin and death and bear them away, a suffering *pro nobis*, but strictly a solidarity in suffering that finally leaves us mired in our sin and death. Unfortunately, in this work, she has become so unmoored from the Christian narrative that the problem of sin and death we see revealed in Christ's death and going to the dead are no longer problematic for Rambo. Sin and death are not overcome in the descent into hell. Instead, God joins humanity in the abyss, lovingly sharing our despair and powerlessness.

I imagine that Rambo would be untroubled by this Chalcedonian critique, given that the person of Christ matters very little to her pneumatology of remaining. What remains beyond the trauma of the cross is a weary Spirit of love that trickles on and persists in the wake of death. This is what remains of theology when she has finished reading it through her "lens of trauma," a weary witness of

---

44. Rambo, *Spirit and Trauma*, 71–72.
45. Rambo, *Spirit and Trauma*, 172.
46. Rambo, *Spirit and Trauma*, 170.

love. This is a wonderfully descriptive, albeit incomplete, anthropology to embrace in the aftermath of trauma, but an utterly hopeless theology. In no way would I disagree that the lens of trauma correctly views this world as a Holy Saturday world. This world is a space where the remainder of death persists in life. Yet, this is a thoroughly dismal theological claim if God simply identifies with our hopelessness and remains mired in our death and trauma.

More to the point though, it is not so much that Rambo's theology, in the end, is hopeless. It is that, in ignoring the resurrection of Jesus Christ in favor of a weary witness of love, she has made a clean break with one of the central claims of the Christian tradition. It is hard to imagine a much different ending, given her methodological starting point. Her work is rather brilliantly and creatively executed from start to finish. Unfortunately, as we saw in chapter 2, there is no way to view the cross as anything other than a meaningless tragedy except from the lens of the resurrection. If she had remained less suspicious and more faithful in her reading of Balthasar and perhaps turned to Barth and others, she might have seen that it is only in light of the resurrection that the hiddenness and darkness of Holy Saturday and Christ's descent into hell can be seen as revealing the fullness of God's love in Christ. Unbound from the resurrection, there is nothing revelatory about Christ's cross or grave. There is not even a weary witness to love, but rather meaninglessness and failure.

Rambo's theological concern for those who live between death and life after trauma remains valid, even though trauma is not a useful hermeneutical lens through which to do such theological work. Holy Saturday is certainly fertile theological ground from which to minister to those who have experienced trauma and suffered the soul wounds of war. To read the story of Holy Saturday without the witness of Easter Sunday, however, is to sow the soil with salt and render it theologically useless from the outset. What might it look like to take seriously the claims of psychology about trauma and the theological insights of the Holy Saturday theology of Balthasar on their own terms when ordered explicitly according to the Chalcedonian pattern?

## Combat Trauma as a Soul Wound

Traumatic events certainly result in very distressing psychological symptoms. Nightmares, daytime hallucinations, and a constant hyper-vigilance dedicated to avoiding any stimuli that might trigger any such terrifying re-experiencing responses are horrific in their own right. Yet, as discussed in chapter 1, for many soldiers, it is the soul wounding that results from trauma that is more deeply troubling than the symptoms of PTSD. As psychiatrist Judith Herman suggests, traumatic events "undermine the belief systems that give meaning to human experience. They violate the victim's faith in a natural or divine order and cast the victim into a state of existential crisis."[47] In response to the suicide of Marine Lieutenant Lewis Puller, Vietnam veteran and son of Marine General "Chesty" Puller and fellow Vietnam veteran Tom Edmunds wrote the following: "'God! God, I'm tired of this shit! This is enough! No more! Please God! No more.' . . . But God doesn't answer, he never did; not then, not now."[48] At war and at home, the hiddenness of God for survivors of combat trauma is, perhaps, the most agonizing reality. On the other side of combat trauma, many soldiers continue to experience a deep and abiding sense of the absence of God. It is from the bottom of this seemingly bottomless pit that such cries of lament pour forth.

Before combat trauma can be understood as a soul wound, clarity is required with respect to what is meant by the "soul." Barth's definition is found in the context of his discussion of the cure of souls. He writes:

> In the language of the Bible and that of Christian understanding the term "soul" (nephesh, and sometimes ruach, ψυχή, and occasionally πνεῦμα) means *the totality of a human being in his individual personal existence*, and therefore this or that man in his unique and incomparable individuality *grounded in the fact that as this or that*

---

47. Herman, *Trauma and Recovery*, 51.

48. Edmonds, *The Way of Bamboo*, quoted in Shay, *Odysseus in America*, 181.

> man he is *the object of the love of God* which is not merely universal but particular in its universality, and therefore of the promise and claim of God which are not merely general but wholly specific; that he is a creature of the Spirit of God quickening and sustaining him.[49]

The soul, then, in Christian theology, is not an immortal, immaterial substance capable of being divorced from embodied reality as in Platonic philosophy. As noted above, for Barth, the soul is always embodied and the body is always besouled. That is to say, to speak of the "soul" is to speak of the totality of a person, specifically as "the object of the love of God." Simply put, the soul is the whole person in relation to God.

To speak of combat trauma as a soul wound is to speak of it as a wound of the whole person in relation to God. Simultaneously, combat trauma is also appropriately the object of study by psychology and may also be conceptualized as a psychological wound. PTSD and other trauma related disorders have been fixtures in the *Diagnostic and Statistical Manual of Mental Disorders* since the third edition and major updates have been included for the most recent fifth edition.[50] Following the Chalcedonian pattern, soul wounds and psychological wounds may be conceptualized in the two distinct language worlds of theology and psychology. Hunsinger writes:

> Theology and psychology represent material that cannot be integrated into a unified whole. They are logically diverse; they have different aims, subject matters, methods, and linguistic conventions. They do not exist on the same level. Both perspectives are fully a part of the pastoral counselor, that is, they are integrated into the *person*, but as language and thought worlds, they are not to be integrated *with one another* in any systematic way.[51]

---

49. Barth, *CD*, 4.3.2:885, emphasis added.
50. See *DSM-V*, 271–80.
51. Hunsinger, *Pastoral Counseling*, 61.

Hunsinger's work is addressed to pastoral counselors who are fluent in both the languages of theology and therapeutic psychology. Even so, it is equally important for all pastoral caregivers to properly relate the two modes of discourse no matter how well-versed they are in either. This requires a careful application of the Chalcedonian pattern to a discussion of soul wounds.

The soul and soul wounds are, theologically, the object of salvation, while psychological wounds are the object of psychotherapeutic healing. There is, therefore, an indissoluble distinction between soul wounds and psychological wounds as they function in these two distinct conceptual language worlds. There is also an inseparable unity. Soul wounds and psychological wounds of trauma occur simultaneously in one person. There is no way to separate these wounds. They are integrally related in the life of a person who has come home from war. Finally, there is an asymmetrical ordering between the psychotherapeutic interventions aimed at treating PTSD and the grace of God made manifest in pastoral care. Psychotherapeutic interventions cannot provide salvation or grace, but the healing they offer can point toward it, albeit usually unknowingly.

Hunsinger, using Barth, unpacks the distinction between salvation and healing by distinguishing between the theological concept of "sin" and the psychological concept of "neurosis" or "victim."[52] It is helpful to reprint her chart noting the differences here.[53]

---

52. Hunsinger, *Pastoral Counseling*, 70–75.

53. This chart is found in Hunsinger, *Pastoral Counseling*, 71. The chart developed by Deborah Hunsinger, in which she relates the status of sinners to the status of victims of childhood abuse or deprivation, is adapted from George Hunsinger's original development of these distinctions. See his seminal essay, Hunsinger, "The Sinner and the Victim," 433–39.

| Sinner | Victim (of childhood abuse or deprivation) |
|---|---|
| 1. Universal category. ("All have sinned and fall short of the glory of God.") | 1. Particular category. (Not all children have "good-enough" parenting.) |
| 2. The sinner qua sinner is culpable. | 2. The victim qua victim is innocent. |
| 3. An "essential" characteristic. | 3. A "non-essential" or "accidental" characteristic. |
| 4. A theological category. | 4. A psychoanalytic or family-systems category. Empirically describable. |
| 5. Only God can save from sin. | 5. Human effort may bring healing or improvement. |
| 6. Sin fosters illusion. People actively complicit in sin. | 6. Victimization has potential to foster insight. Victims complicit only by adapting to dysfunctional system. |
| 7. Salvation is an essentially eternal resolution. | 7. Healing is an essentially this-world resolution. |

While the language of victim is now largely passé—in favor of the more empowering designation of survivor—the basic point is the same. Whether a victim or survivor, something has happened to someone. She is the victim of that happening, that is, it happened to her, and perhaps we might say on the other side of the event she is now a survivor. The language of victim/survivor is readily applicable to those who experience combat trauma. In terms of Hunsinger's chart, the psychological characteristics of survivors of combat trauma can be outlined thusly: (1) survivors of combat trauma are a particular subset of combat veterans. Not all combat soldiers experience trauma. (2) It may be more difficult to sort out whether the "victim qua victim is innocent." To be sure, war is fraught with moral complexity. Nevertheless, it might tentatively be asserted that, in the particularity of a specific encounter with trauma, the soldier is innocent, even if that same soldier also perpetrated traumatic acts of violence upon the very enemy that traumatized him. That is, a moral distinction should be made between traumatic acts witnessed or experienced (survived) and similar such acts inflicted upon the enemy (or innocents) such that even if moral responsibility may be demanded of soldiers for the acts they commit (even lawful acts committed under orders), they are not responsible for the moral behavior of the enemy. (3) Surviving trauma is a "non-essential" or "accidental" characteristic. (4) Trauma is empirically describable, especially in light of recent neurobiological findings. (5) There are well-documented treatment modalities for providing healing after trauma. (6) There may even be post-traumatic growth.[54] (7) Recovery after trauma is focused on symptom reduction or living with persistent symptoms. Viewed from the language world of psychology, victims or survivors of combat trauma have psychological wounds that are properly the object of psychotherapeutic intervention.

To speak of soul wounds—wounds of the whole person in relation to God—is to enter the theological language world of sin and salvation. The experience of combat trauma and the attending overwhelming evil are often followed by the experience of the profound silence of God. The fundamental question "why?" echoes back seemingly unanswered. God's absence or malignancy is often presumed. For combat trauma survivors, this encounter with the hiddenness of God often leads to a loss of faith.[55]

In terms of Hunsinger's chart above, (1 and 3) the survivor of combat trauma is, of course, also a sinner—not necessarily *qua* survivor/victim, but sinner nonetheless, as a member of the human family (Rom 3:23). (2) As a sinner, the combat survivor is certainly culpable. (4) The combat survivor as sinner is only seen as such in light of the Word of the cross and it is sin that prevents the hearing of that Word (and no psychology can discern it).[56] (5)

54. See Calhoun and Tedeschi, *Posttraumatic Growth*.

55. Faith here should be understood as *fides qua creditur*, the faith with which we believe, rather than *fides quae creditur*, the faith which we believe.

56. For a discussion of the limits of psychology in preaching forgiveness

The soul wounds of trauma are wounds in relationship to God and can only be overcome by God. (6) The hiddenness of God in the aftermath of trauma is an illusion fostered by the overwhelming encounter with evil. This illusion is so impactful because it is so very near the truth at the heart of the gospel. It is this lie that prevents the hearing of the good news. It is indeed *through* the hiddenness of the cross and grave that God's grace is revealed. (7) The salvific healing of soul wounds is a result of the grace that God has shown humanity in choosing to be God in Christ for us from all eternity. Salvation is revealed in time and fulfilled in eternity.

The soul wound of combat trauma is the seeming eclipse of God's presence by horrific trauma and death. In the wake of such occurrences, it is as if the light of God's love has been blotted out by a sometimes very literal ash cloud of death and evil. Certainly, moral ambiguities abound on the battlefield. Traumatic events are often a result of the evil inflicted upon soldiers by the enemy. So too soldiers, acting as the instrumentality of the state or on their own, bring death and trauma upon the enemy (and too often innocents). Even when strict rules of engagement are enforced, war tends toward inhumanity and injustice. In the chaos and terror of battle, many soldiers act in brutal and dehumanizing ways. The fact that soldiers wrestle with matters of conscience relating to their experience on the battlefield reflects the resilience of their humanity in the face of the dehumanizing nature of war. This struggle of conscience has come to be known as moral injury. It results from "perpetrating, failing to prevent, bearing witness to, or learning about acts that transgress deeply held moral beliefs and expectations."[57] The impediment to hearing the gospel created by moral injury is not simply the encounter with the sin of others, but also being brought face to face with one's own capacity for evil. In the former, the light of God's love is seemingly blotted out by the

and sin see Bonhoeffer, *Spiritual Care*, 35–36.

57. Litz et al., "Moral Injury," 700. See also the more recent monograph outlining a treatment model in Litz et al., *Adaptive Disclosure*. For a critique of this model as a form of "therapeutic instrumentalism," see Kinghorn, "Combat Trauma," 57–74.

darkness of evil. In the latter, self-condemnation prevents the reception of God's love because of felt personal unworthiness.[58] The fact of having killed another human being haunts the imagination and causes ongoing moral anguish. The result of traumatic and morally injurious experiences in combat is the same; they create an impediment to hearing the good news of the gospel and leave the person feeling abandoned by God.

## Conclusion

In Exodus 17, the Israelites are in the desert on the other side of their Red Sea deliverance and yet they have no water and are dying of thirst. Faced with the prospect of death in the desert, they wonder whether perhaps life in Egypt would have been better. In the absence of help and hope they wonder, "Is the Lord among us or not?" (Exod 17:7). Combat trauma and moral injury confront survivors with the compelling urgency of just that question. The answer to this question cannot be revealed by psychology or trauma theory or trauma *per se* (*contra* Rambo), rather, it is found in the gospel that it is precisely in hiddenness that God is revealed. This is the unsearchable wisdom of Holy Saturday that Jesus Christ, very God, is abandoned by God *pro nobis*. The experience of God's hiddenness is undoubtedly a sign of our separation from God in sin, but, foremost, it is a faint witness to Christ's own experience of forsakenness. It is faint because the full-measure of that cup has been drunk only by him and foremost because Christ's solidarity with our forsakenness is precisely how God has chosen to reveal himself. As Balthasar put it so well in chapter 2 (and it bears repeating): "He wanted to sink so low that, in the future, all falling would be a falling into him, and every streamlet of bitterness and despair would henceforth run down into his lowermost abyss."[59]

---

58. For an examination of self-condemnation and self-forgiveness from the perspective of clinical psychology see Worthington and Langberg, "Religious Considerations," 274–88.

59. Balthasar, *Heart of the World*, 43.

Because Christ descended into hell, no matter how far combat veterans fall, they fall into God's love. For those who know in equal measure that "war is hell" and "coming home is hell" too, this is good news indeed. We turn now to the proclamation of this good news in the context of spiritual care.

# 4

# Coming Home from the Far Country

I WAS SITTING IN on a substance abuse group when the call came on the duty phone. Michael was on the other side of the inpatient psychiatric floor and wanted to speak with a chaplain. When I arrived, I immediately recognized him from the previous day. I had sat in on a group therapy session with him. We had connected around serving in the same area of operations in Afghanistan.[1] He had just turned twenty-one and was already married. He had come all the way from Fort Drum, New York to receive inpatient, and then outpatient therapy at Fort Belvoir Community Hospital in Virginia. We made our way to the meditation room on the far end of the floor to talk. I could tell he was in great distress. As his story began to unfold, I was glad to have already established a relationship with him. It was likely that prior relationship had increased enough trust for him to risk sharing:

---

1. As I recounted in chapter 1, I served in the Arghandab District of Kandahar Province, Afghanistan from June 2010–May 2011. He served in the neighboring Zhari District from March 2011–February 2012. While we did not serve in the same district, the terrain, culture, religion, population density, agriculture, and daily rhythm of life were nearly identical. Most significantly, his unit faced the same sort of combat with the Taliban that mine had encountered.

> I was in the tower on top of the OP [observation post] while the patrol was out. I was manning the Mark 19.[2] I could see the patrol. I could also see the men with rifles. I called up to my lieutenant and he cleared me to fire. They were getting ready to ambush the patrol. It wasn't just men though. There were some kids playing nearby. I fired anyway. Dozens of 40 mm rounds rained down on their position. When the dust settled, they [the kids] were gone. The kids were just playing. I was given a certificate of achievement for saving the patrol from ambush. I never told anyone about the kids. I've been living in hell ever since.[3]

I was honored to hear this young man's painful story. He had been admitted to treat PTSD, with which he undoubtedly struggled. It was also clear that what had brought him to this moment of distress was not what happened to him (trauma), but his assessment of what he had done (moral injury), potentially killing innocent children at play. As he put it, he had been "living in hell" ever since. Although he did not profess faith in God, his distress belied an embedded theology with features of sin and judgment (and no hint of grace). As a result of his self-condemnation, shame, and guilt, this soldier could barely hold his own child or share intimacy with his wife without recognizing some repulsive contradiction in himself. He felt unworthy to go on living and unworthy of the significant loving relationships he had with his wife and child. Michael was stuck in the far country. Trauma and moral injury had crippled him to the point of hospitalization. He certainly benefited from the psychotherapeutic interventions that were applied. Indeed, with his risk for suicide, his life depended upon the safety and structure he found there. Yet, what hope is there for Michael and others like

---

2. The Mark 19 is a belt-fed automatic 40 mm grenade launcher. It can effectively fire 60 rounds per minute on a point target up to 1,500 meters with impressive impact up to 2,200 meters. It is an extremely deadly weapon system.

3. This is an excerpt of a pastoral conversation with an inpatient active duty soldier at Fort Belvoir Community Hospital, Fort Belvoir, VA, December 17, 2012.

him who are "living in hell" after coming home from war? And what can pastors and chaplains do to bear witness to such hope?

In chapter 3, Shelly Rambo's theology of remaining was outlined. She suggests that theology be reformed in response to trauma. Indeed, she argues that trauma might be the lens through which to do theology. She concludes that, in the aftermath of trauma, the Spirit remains as a weary witness to love.[4] She grants trauma (or trauma theory) priority in her reading. Thus, perhaps it could be said that God bears death with us, but God does not bear it away. Her methodology was seen to be inadequate in light of Hunsinger's use of the Chalcedonian pattern. The interest of this work is a theology of Holy Saturday that takes seriously both cross *and* resurrection. In chapter 3, I also outlined the experience of God's hiddenness after trauma and moral injury as soul wounds distinct from the psychological symptoms of PTSD. It is these soul wounds that are the unique concern of pastors and chaplains. In this chapter, a Chalcedonian approach to spiritual care of trauma will be outlined. The psychological care suggested by Judith Herman's stages of recovery will be seen as an analogical witness to the spiritual care that might be offered. Luke's parable of the prodigal son will provide the framework. In the end, it will be shown that a theology of Holy Saturday provides an authentic place from which to bear witness to the beautiful mystery of God's presence and love in the midst of death, trauma, and the often hellish realities of coming home from war.

## Herman's Stages of Recovery

While the conceptual mooring of the spiritual care of the soul wounds of war must remain firmly tied to theology—specifically a theology of Holy Saturday—the healing offered by psychotherapeutic interventions can function as a sign that points toward salvation. I find the work of Judith Herman to be such a sign. In *Trauma and Recovery*, she outlines recovery as following along a

---

4. Rambo, *Spirit and Trauma*, 170.

trajectory of safety, remembrance and mourning, and reconnection. Herman suggests that these stages are not rigidly linear and that patients may oscillate as issues that were thought to have been addressed arise again. Nevertheless, the stages provide a general shape and direction of recovery as patients move from "unpredictable danger to reliable safety, from dissociated trauma to acknowledged memory, and from stigmatized isolation to restored social connection."[5]

## Safety

The initial tasks that Herman outlines for therapists working with traumatized patients is to establish a healing relationship of trust.[6] If trauma has resulted in disconnection and distrust, therapists in relationship with trauma survivors seek to foster their reestablishment. This begins when patients are able to recognize they have a problem and courageously seek help. Therapists must often gently nurture them toward this end with reassurances that the symptoms they are experiencing are normal responses to extreme circumstances. The experience of trauma and the symptoms that follow rob survivors of a sense of control over their own bodies and the world around them. When trauma is untreated, the traumatized often seek control through self-destructive behaviors and habits.[7] It is important in this phase to help patients regain a sense of control over both their bodies and environment. This is done for the body through the reestablishment of healthy sleep, diet, and exercise habits. In addition, symptom reduction is pursued through a regime of medication (as prescribed), stress management, and relaxation techniques.[8]

---

5. Herman, *Trauma and Recovery*, 155.

6. Herman, *Trauma and Recovery*, 133.

7. In addition to self-medication with drugs and alcohol, some of these destructive behaviors may even include symbolic or literal re-enactments of the traumatic event. See Herman, *Trauma and Recovery*, 37–42.

8. Herman, *Trauma and Recovery*, 158–60.

A patient's important relationships must also be assessed as possible sources of emotional and practical support during treatment or even danger. Throughout this period, the therapist must continually emphasize to the patient that the journey of recovery from trauma is akin to running a marathon. It is the survivor who must run the race, with the therapist serving as coach and cheerleader. At the end of this phase, the patient's symptoms will be under control, supportive relationships will be in place, and he or she will feel less isolated and a little more trusting. Once this foundation of safety is in place, the patient is ready to address the memory of trauma.[9]

## Remembrance and Mourning

In this second stage, the task is to help the survivor of trauma retell her story. The choice to speak the unspeakable remains with the patient; the therapist stands ready as witness and ally. The focus here is to bring detail and depth to the trauma in its retelling so it can ultimately be integrated into the patient's larger life story. Nonverbal or indirect means of communication may be employed, including drawing, painting, or writing, when the most painful moments of trauma are addressed. The goal, however, is for patients to give voice to their story. Written communication and drawings must be verbalized eventually. Reconstruction of the story is not simply a descriptive act. It must also include what the patient felt. Throughout this phase, the therapist must help the patient seek balance because "avoiding the traumatic memories leads to stagnation in the recovery process, while approaching them too precipitately leads to fruitless and damaging reliving of the trauma."[10]

On the other side of this reconstructed trauma, the patient must then begin to wrestle with the meaning of the event. "Why?" "Why me?" Herman writes: "She stands mute before the

---

9. Herman, *Trauma and Recovery*, 174.
10. Herman, *Trauma and Recovery*, 176.

emptiness of evil, feeling the insufficiency of any known system of explanation."[11] The survivor is challenged to examine the values and beliefs she once held and begin to reconstruct a response that struggles with the moral questions of guilt and responsibility. This is not merely a cognitive exercise, but should lead the survivor toward action. What must be done in light of the traumatic event? The therapist, in this phase, does not provide answers, but helps give voice to the questions and the struggle beyond them. Herman suggests that the therapist *qua* witness stands in moral solidarity with the patient. Witnessing trauma involves taking sides and taking a stand against evil with the survivor of trauma.[12]

Loss is inherent to trauma. Thus, the telling of the trauma story will undoubtedly arouse deep grief. Whether the loss is a loved one, a limb, or an understanding of self and world, mourning traumatic loss is an indispensable part of the healing process. Often patients are resistant to mourning, fearing there will be no end to grief once they begin. Rather than grieve, many patients may choose to dwell on fantasies of "magical resolution through revenge, forgiveness, or compensation."[13] Ultimately, the survivor must reckon with the fact that neither revenge, nor forgiveness, nor compensation will erase the trauma. The only way forward is through the pain of mourning. If the survivor perseveres in her work toward recovery, eventually, she will realize "the story is a memory like other memories, and it begins to fade as other memories do. Her grief, too, begins to lose its vividness. It occurs to the survivor that perhaps the trauma is not the most important or even the most interesting part of her life."[14] The goal is that the survivor may again find energy and hope.

---

11. Herman, *Trauma and Recovery*, 178.
12. Herman, *Trauma and Recovery*, 7.
13. Herman, *Trauma and Recovery*, 189.
14. Herman, *Trauma and Recovery*, 195.

## Reconnection

Herman outlines the third stage of recovery from trauma as reconnection with ordinary life. In this stage, the therapist is concerned with helping to foster the reconnection of the patient with herself and other significant relationships that may have suffered posttrauma. As Herman notes, here, the survivor of trauma must work to develop a new self and new or renewed relationships.[15] The creation of a new self is an exercise in imagination and honesty. The therapist invites the patient to hope, dream, and play with her future. The patient can be proud of what she has overcome and accomplished, but honest self-examination should be encouraged and limitations acknowledged. At this point in recovery, the survivor has a renewed ability to trust and is ready to invest more deeply in relationships based on mutuality and healthy boundaries. Here she may acknowledge the various levels of support that sustained her through the work of recovery.

Through the course of the therapeutic journey, some may be inspired to sublimate their traumatic experience into the pursuit of a survivor mission. In addition to the personal nature of their trauma, these survivors may be gripped by the larger social, political, or religious connections it contains that impel them toward some form of response. Such responses often take the form of public witness against atrocities and pursuing justice. Herman warns, "Resolution of the trauma is never final; recovery is never complete."[16] Nevertheless, if pursued, the task of recovery may eventually become subordinate to the enjoyment of life, meaningful work, and loving relationships.

## The Return of the Prodigal

In chapter 1, I suggested that, like the prodigal son, soldiers who return home from combat or have suffered trauma often remain

---

15. Herman, *Trauma and Recovery*, 196.
16. Herman, *Trauma and Recovery*, 211.

stuck in the far country. This dislocation is a result of the symptoms of PTSD and morally injurious experiences that cut them off from the people they once were and the family and friends that care very deeply for them. More significantly, though, it is the experience of feeling cut off from and abandoned by God. Living in this hell, veterans often exile themselves to the margins of society.[17] Luke 15 suggests a form for the spiritual care of those who suffer the far-country dislocation of combat trauma and it is analogous to Herman's stages of recovery. I suggest that the spiritual care of the soul wound of combat trauma can be focused around the practices of sanctuary, lament and confession, and forgiveness and reconciliation. Like Herman's stages, there is movement along a trajectory from sanctuary to lament and confession to forgiveness and reconciliation, but they should not be understood as strictly linear.

## Sanctuary

In the parable, the son—while hungry and wallowing in filth—remembers, "How many of my father's hired hands have bread enough and to spare, but here I am dying of hunger!" (Luke 15:17). This points us toward the mission of the church to provide sanctuary for those who bear soul wounds. Sanctuary means the church provides refuge for those who have been left wandering in a foreign land. Cities of refuge or sanctuary cities, for the protection of those who commit manslaughter, are prescribed by the Priestly and Deuteronomic traditions in Numbers 35 and Deuteronomy 19, respectively. Sanctuary is also a concept in medieval law in England and various places in continental Europe that dates back to fourth century Roman law. It was available to those who might otherwise face the death penalty.[18] These laws suggest the church as a place of safety for those with nowhere else to turn. In the end,

---

17. This dislocation can be literal as well as psychological and spiritual. It is not surprising that veterans suffer homelessness at twice the rate of the general population and that a majority of homeless veterans suffer from PTSD. See Eve B. Carlson et al., "Homeless Veterans," 970.

18. See Jordan, "Medieval Sanctuary," 17–32.

though, it is God who is our refuge. The Psalms are replete with such imagery for God (Ps 18:2, Ps 46:1, Ps 71:3, and Ps 91:2). The tabernacle or temple itself may be the physical location of such refuge (Ps 27:5), especially the altar (Exod 21:14, 1 Kgs 1:50, and 1 Kgs 2:28). These images find their fulfillment in Christ as both high priest and sacrifice upon the heavenly altar (Rom 3:25 and Heb 4–10).[19] Indeed, it is as the one who descended into hell that Jesus now sits at the right hand of the Father as our intercessor. Jesus is priest, altar, sacrifice, and true sanctuary for all in need of refuge. Yet, at first, for those who bear the soul wounds of combat trauma or moral injury, the hiddenness of God—or even the fear of a malignant God—seems to preclude seeking and finding refuge in God's presence. Even so, pastors, chaplains, and others may stand in as representatives of the church who bear witness to the actuality of such sanctuary, even if it may still seem impossible to the survivor of combat trauma.

Sanctuary means that the church and her ministers provide a safe and sacred space in which the soul-wounded can tell their stories. This often requires the help of psychiatrists and others so that the symptoms of PTSD can be reduced enough for such work to begin. Beyond medication, it is the love and compassion of another human being that is necessary for such horrific and painful stories to be told. As Deborah Hunsinger writes:

> Those who seek to reclaim their lives after trauma need to face what has actually happened to them. *It requires their attention.* If their nervous system is in a hyperaroused state, they need to find as much safety as possible. Only true safety will provide the emotional security needed to begin the healing process commonly known as mourning. Giving voice to all that they have experienced—the terror and helplessness, the sense of moral outrage and personal violation, the sorrow, hurt, anger, and grief—becomes the essential first step in piecing together a coherent narrative.

---

19. For an excellent analysis of the cultic and priestly language in reference to Jesus Christ see Barth, *CD*, 4.1:274–83.

> Yet none of this can happen apart from the lively presence of *a caring other*. Who can bear the anguish of such a narrative, without minimizing or denying it, without giving advice or offering strategies to overcome it? Who can listen without offering empty platitudes or switching the focus to a similar story of their own? Who has the wisdom to refrain from asking intrusive questions prompted by their own anxiety, allowing the traumatized person space to tell his story in his own way at his own pace? Who can offer a compassionate, caring presence, free of pity or sympathy, free of judgment, praise or blame?
>
> Healing begins as the traumatized begin to piece together a coherent narrative, creating a web of meaning around unspeakable events while remaining fully connected emotionally both to themselves and to their listener.[20]

Both therapists and pastoral caregivers require a relationship of trust and the establishment of safety as a foundation for the work they do. This is paramount for the creation of a coherent narrative after trauma. As such, pastors have much to learn in conversation with those who practice psychotherapy. Furthermore, if survivors of trauma are at risk of hurting themselves or are unable to tell their story because they need medication or clinical treatment, pastoral caregivers have a duty to get them to the help they need. Professional interdisciplinary care is not just a good idea but often a matter of life and death as well.

Luke's parable continues: "So he set off and went to his father. But, while he was still far off, his father saw him and was filled with compassion; he ran and put his arms around him and kissed him" (Luke 15:20). The difference between therapy and spiritual care is that spiritual care is done in the presence of *the* Father. This is what the concept of sanctuary ultimately suggests, a holy presence. The soul-wounded seek out pastoral care not simply in search of good listeners who care about them, although pastors should

---

20. Hunsinger, *Bearing the Unbearable*, 10–11.

do those things. They come for pastoral care because of the holy nature of the office. While trust and safety are essential in the context of pastoral care, ultimately, they come not from the pastor or chaplain, but the One to whom the caregiver bears witness. From a Chalcedonian perspective, the safety sought in psychotherapy is a sign that points beyond itself to the refuge or sanctuary found ultimately in God. Dietrich Bonhoeffer writes:

> All questions of personal worthiness are beside the point and put us in the realm of psychotherapy. To those who come to us for spiritual care, our ability has less than no authority. Only the mission binds us and calls us together. The pastor as spiritual curate is not a person of unusual experience, ability, or maturity. He should not pass himself off as such, as a "person you can trust," "a priestly person," or the like. If he does, he will only put himself in Jesus's place and arouse expectations he will of necessity disappoint.[21]

Pastors are to place the traumatized before God alone; this is the nature of our office. Even so, Bonhoeffer acknowledges that the task of spiritual care begins with listening. He writes, "The pastor's task is to listen and the parishioner's is to talk. The pastor's duty in this form of spiritual care may be to be silent for a long time."[22] Eduard Thurneysen also acknowledges that pastoral care is carried out in conversation. In *A Theology of Pastoral Care* he suggests: "This form is not accidental, but constitutes the very nature of this means. It is a conversation both formally and materially."[23] Conversation is the very nature of pastoral care because in it we are invited to respond to the Word of God spoken to us in our particularity.

Indeed, pastors are acutely interested and concerned about the Word of God spoken to the particular one for whom they care. At the very outset of his study, Thurneysen says that pastoral care

---

21. Bonhoeffer, *Spiritual Care*, 37.
22. Bonhoeffer, *Spiritual Care*, 31.
23. Thurneysen, *Pastoral Care*, 102.

is "the communication of the Word of God to individuals."²⁴ Karl Barth explains that communication this way:

> Here, too, the general includes rather than excludes the particular, i.e., the turning of one brother to another, or to one who is not yet a brother but may be claimed as such only *in spe*, as this is actualized concretely and specifically in fulfillment of the ministry of the community. The cure of souls understood in this special sense as the individual cure of souls means a concrete actualization of the participation of the one in the particular past, present and future of the other, in his particular burdens and afflictions, but, above all, in his particular promise and hope in the singularity of his existence as created and sustained by God. It means the active interest of the one in the divine calling and therefore in the being and nature of this specific other.²⁵

Pastoral caregivers are deeply concerned for the brother or sister who stands before them, his or her past, present, and future burdens, pain, and, most importantly, hope found in God. This hope is grounded in the divine calling. Pastors and those who come home from war are invited to stand upon it alone. Thus Hunsinger suggests that:

> All pastoral care depends upon prayer, leads to worship, and trusts in the promises of God. Such an orientation leads us to confess that though we ourselves, with our enduring failures to love, cannot truly redeem traumatic loss, we cling in hope to the One who can and does.²⁶

Pastors and chaplains stand equally in need of grace and must trust—along with those for whom they care—that God in Christ bears the soul wounds of trauma and indeed has borne them away. Pastors must lovingly listen to the stories of those who bear the wounds of combat trauma in light of this hope.

---

24. Thurneysen, *Pastoral Care*, 11.
25. Barth, *CD*, 4.3.2:885–86.
26. Hunsinger, *Bearing the Unbearable*, 2.

## Lament and Confession

For the therapist, the task in the second stage is to help combat veterans re-narrate their story so that the trauma is relocated in the past within the larger story of their life. It is a task of remembrance and mourning.[27] Just as therapists invite their patients to return to painful memories of the past to open up space for envisioning a future, the pastoral caregiver invites the combat veteran to see her trauma in light of the trauma of the cross and Christ's descent into hell. Christ goes before us and with us, as a brother pointing us to the Father. Through the tears of her grief and the grief of the cross, she may be able to catch glimpses of a new future and a true home. This does not mean that horrific trauma is then tied up neatly, wrapped with a bow, and set aside. Grief is lifelong because loss is lifelong and, thus, lament, too, may be lifelong.

With his cry from the cross, "My God, my God, why have you forsaken me?" (Mark 15:34), Jesus brings lamentation not just to the heart of the New Testament,[28] but to the center of authentic Christian faith.[29] In the foreword to Ann Weems's *Psalms of Lament*, Walter Brueggemann writes: "For like the life of this poet, the life of the world is saturated with pain and ache not yet finished, not yet answered, not yet resolved. And we are left with the demanding question, What shall we do with so much of the hurt that is left unfinished?"[30] Brueggemann suggests lament. The Psalms provide us both words with which to cry out our hurt and pain to God as well as potential form. They give order to our grief.

In chapter 2, Psalm 88 was lifted up as a witness in Scripture where those who suffer the Holy Saturday experience after trauma may find their experience of God's hiddenness mirrored back.

---

27. Herman, *Trauma and Recovery*, 175.
28. Campbell, "NT Lament," 757–60.
29. Robert Dykstra suggests that the rending of the temple curtain is God's act of lament at the death of Jesus. This rending is an act against God-self that exposes the fullness of God. Lament for God and humans leads to greater vulnerability. See Dykstra, "Rending the Curtain," 59–69.
30. Brueggemann, Foreword to *Psalms of Lament*, ix.

More than that though, in praying the lamentations of Scripture, we join Christ in prayer, for Christ has cast his lot fully with us taking upon himself all sin and evil upon the cross. Brueggemann argues that the Psalms of lament may contain the following six elements. (1) Lament begins by naming God. It is an intimate form of address. Lament is indeed prayer addressed to God. Even as it rises up out of deep pain and anguish, even the experience of abandonment by God is nevertheless a prayer addressed to God in faith. (2) In the Psalms of lament, Israel brings her complaint to God. God's failure to act and the trouble that resulted are set out. (3) In light of the complaint, a petition is made for God's rescue. (4) This petition is bolstered by attempts to motivate God to act by means of repentance or by appeals to God's honor. (5) The imprecatory Psalms even include petitions for God's vengeance upon enemies. Placing vengeance in God's hands alone removes the Psalmist from the circle of violence begetting violence. Read Christologically, the Psalms suggest that all persons stand before God as enemies. (6) Finally, nearly all of the Psalms—Psalm 88 being the exception—include a change of mood at the end. They close with praise and rejoicing and a note of confidence at being heard by God.[31]

Lamentation is a courageous act of faith. Protest, anger, grief, disappointment, and profound sadness are laid out before God. Lament in the Old Testament pours forth from the lips of psalmists and prophets alike. When Job opens his mouth, he curses the day of his birth (Job 3). Jeremiah mourns for his homeland and his people, even as he has been charged with delivering the word of their destruction (Jer 8:18—9:2). Lament is honest speech amidst suffering; nevertheless it is speech addressed to God. To address our suffering to God grounds our experience in something or, rather, in Someone who transcends it. It is important to highlight that pastors do not stand at a distance from those for whom they care. Just as we join Christ in his prayers of lament as he, in solidarity, has joined us, so too do pastors also join in the "deafening

---

31. Brueggemann, Foreword to *Psalms of Lament*, x–xii.

alleluia / rising from the souls / of those who weep" in prayers of lament. Ann Weems puts it poetically:

> In the godforsaken, obscene quicksand of life,
> there is a deafening alleluia
> rising from the souls
> of those who weep,
> *and of those who weep with those who weep.*
> If you watch, you will see
> the hand of God
> putting the stars back in their skies
> one by one.[32]

Further, the one who laments does so in hope that God will do something new and different ("put the stars back in their skies"). Such hope may be difficult to discern, as in Psalm 88, but the act of addressing God represents more than a last ditch effort when all else has failed. Ann Weems puts it this way: "There is no salvation in self-help books; the help we need is far beyond self. Our only hope is to march ourselves to the throne of God and, in loud lament, cry out the pain that lives in our souls."[33] Soul wounds cut deep, to the core of our being. But, just as in the parable, the best hope of return from the far country is to come into the sanctuary, into the Father's presence, and to address God. As Hunsinger puts it: "We thus facilitate healing when we help the afflicted cry out their sorrow, rage, and tears *to God.* Prayers of lament—crying out to God for deliverance—seem to be faith's only alternative to despair."[34]

When the wounding is the result of the sin of others, the evil we encounter in the trauma of war, the form that address takes is lament. When the wounding is a result of our own sin, the form our address to God takes is confession. For those who are suffering the spiritual wounds of war, both may be required. Lament

---

32. Weems, *Psalms of Lament*, xvii, emphasis added.
33. Weems, *Psalms of Lament*, xvi.
34. Hunsinger, *Bearing the Unbearable*, 17.

and confession are the best responses to sin and evil, our own or that of others, because they keep us in relation to God even as that relationship has been called into question. Indeed, caregiver, survivor, and perpetrator stand before God equally as sinners and, in Christ's descent, God has joined in solidarity with all. Hunsinger writes:

> Indeed, whenever we affirm that Christ died for sinners, we affirm our solidarity with all who do harm, solidarity in sin as well as in our deliverance from sin. In confessing ourselves as sinners, utterly unable to save ourselves, we recognize that under similar circumstances of deprivation, terror or colossal historic evils, we, too, would be capable of monstrous crimes toward our fellow human beings. The cross of Jesus Christ is God's response not only to the terror of human trauma but also the anguish of human guilt, bringing succor and healing to the one, and judgment, forgiveness, and the "godly grief" of repentance to the other (2 Cor 7:10).[35]

In Christ, God has come to bring healing and hope to both those who have suffered trauma and those who have inflicted it upon others. Many who return home from war are in the position of both.

Luke continues with the parable: "Then, the son said to him, 'Father, I have sinned against heaven and before you; I am no longer worthy to be called your son'" (Luke 15:21). This is what Bonhoeffer says about forgiveness:

> The word of forgiveness is invariably a concrete word for concrete sins. If I do not want to hear it concretely because I want to retain this part of my life for myself, I cannot hear the word of forgiveness at all. For every other area in my life I soon turn the Word of God into a drug—and one soon tires of drugs as a rule. The grace of God becomes, in the end, reduced to the grace I grant to myself.[36]

35. Hunsinger, *Bearing the Unbearable*, 14–15.
36. Bonhoeffer, *Spiritual Care*, 33.

As Bonhoeffer puts it, "a concrete word for concrete sins." This is at the very center of spiritual care. The other form of address we must encourage for our soldiers with soul wounds is confession. When we transgress our basic moral identity and violate our most basic beliefs, we must join the prodigal son in saying: "I have sinned against heaven and before you; I am no longer worthy to be called your son." Through confession, we open our ears again to hear God's word of grace. What does this mean in the context of the spiritual wounds of war?

I would suggest that all soul-wounding is a result of very concrete sin and evil. Trauma may come through violence at the hands of another or as a result of terrible accidents and so-called natural evil, such as tsunamis, storms, mudslides, etc. To understand this sin during war requires much discernment. Soldiers are both victims and perpetrators of violence, oftentimes in the same instant. Moreover, in the chaos of combat, failing to save fellow soldiers or innocents can be as spiritually devastating as legally justified acts of killing or even participating in war crimes or atrocities. As we saw in chapter 3, both moral injury and trauma create an impediment to hearing the gospel. Those who suffer the soul wounds of trauma and moral injury may doubt God's goodness, love, or even presence in their lives. On the other side of trauma, those crying out for justice and restoration may lament that God has seemingly abandoned them. After moral injury, those who, like Michael, at the outset of the chapter, perceive themselves as justly condemned to a living hell may feel unworthy of God's love or even believe God to be the author of their damnable plight.

Carson was one of our most capable medics on the battlefield. He provided point of injury care for multiple traumatic amputations and was beloved by his entire company. After returning from leave, he sought behavioral healthcare and all but refused to return to our area of operations. After several months of serving at our battalion's aid station, he finally went back to his platoon. Although he had witnessed as much trauma as anyone in our battalion, it was not fear that held him back. He had shot a boy, perhaps no more than thirteen. This boy had been fighting with the Taliban. This boy had fired an AK-47 at Carson's patrol. Nonetheless, this was a boy and Carson had killed him. Carson's self-judgment pushed him to the brink of suicide. I think that his role as a medic only exacerbated his quandary. His job was to save lives and he had taken the life of a child. On the other hand, John, another one of our medics, had failed to save the life of one of our Explosive Ordinance Disposal technicians. John had worked tirelessly until the medical evacuation flight arrived, but to no avail. John blamed himself. Never mind that, given the severity of the traumatic amputation, even the best trauma surgeon in the world could not have stemmed the deadly flow of blood. For John, this blood was "on his hands" and he, too, wrestled with thoughts of suicide.

Certainly, both of these men were exposed to overwhelming trauma. Yet, PTSD alone does not properly account for the emotional distress and suicidality that followed. Both men had saved many lives and had much for which to be proud. Carson had probably saved the lives of others in his platoon by killing the boy. Both were men of faith and both used explicitly theological language to describe their distress. Both had not only judged themselves unworthy before their fellow soldiers but also, most significantly, before God. The love of God was imperceptible from the pit of guilt and shame in which they found themselves. They were mired in a web of evil and trauma, bearing guilt and death that they could not bear alone. Thankfully, they were held by brothers in arms, who understood and bore their burdens with them (sanctuary). It was the witness of love from caring others that eventually opened them up to hearing anew God's word of grace. Ultimately, only God can bear our sin and death and God, in Jesus, bears it away *pro nobis*. Through lament and confession, we offer up our burdens to the only one who can bear them and, as we do, may come to know that the parable is less about a prodigal son than about a prodigal Father who loves freely.

## Forgiveness and Reconciliation

Herman outlines the third stage of recovery from trauma as reconnection. In this stage, the therapist is concerned with helping to foster reconnection of the patient with the self and other significant relationships that may have suffered post-trauma.[37] These reconnections will also concern pastors and chaplains, but chief in focus will be the culmination of the journey from the far country to home at peace with God. As Herman rightly notes, the survivor of trauma must here work to "develop a new self" and "find anew a sustaining faith," as it was the perceived severing of this tie of faith (*fides qua creditur*) in the event of trauma that left them stranded in the far country.[38] Although lament may be lifelong and confession is only the beginning of a journey, both help those who have suffered spiritual wounds in combat to place their stories before God. It is only in God's presence that these stories can be redeemed. It is only in God's presence that those dislocated in the far country can ultimately find forgiveness and reconciliation.

Here is the amazing response of the father in Jesus's parable:

> But while he was still far off, his father saw him and was filled with compassion; he ran and put his arms around him and kissed him. . . . The father said to his slaves, "Quickly, bring out a robe—the best one—and put it on him; put a ring on his finger and sandals on his feet. And get the fatted calf and kill it, and let us eat and celebrate, for this son of mine was dead and is alive again; he was lost and is found!" And they began to celebrate. (Luke 15:22–24)

The father runs and embraces his son, even before the son can get the words out of his mouth. God's forgiveness is waiting for us before we can even stammer out a confession. As Paul suggests in Romans, even while we were sinners and enemies of God, Jesus, the obedient son, made his way into the far country and descended even to the depths of hell that we might be reconciled with God

---

37. Herman, *Trauma and Recovery*, 196.
38. Herman, *Trauma and Recovery*, 196.

(Rom 5:6–11). Indeed, it is as the One who has "descended into hell" and "sits at the right hand of God the Father Almighty" that Christ joins those who cry out before the throne of grace. Hunsinger suggests that it is Christ bearing the unbearable that is ultimately good news for those who suffer unbearable trauma:

> At its core, the cross becomes gospel for the traumatized only if they are able to see there a *divine love* willing to bear what is unbearable for mortal, fallen human beings. God bears for us the full weight of both sin and death. If God in Jesus Christ descends into the worst hell imaginable in order to deliver us from the hells we inflict upon one another, then such a God is worthy of our trust. We need not stand by helplessly witnessing the suffering and dying of those we love; we have a God to whom we can entrust them in life and in death. For Jesus Christ is not simply a human companion who comforts us by suffering trauma alongside us. As the creeds of the church attest, he is known to us as the risen Lord, the very Wisdom and Power of God, through whom God will fulfill his purpose of redemption. Jesus Christ, the gospel attests, bears what cannot be borne by fragile, fallen human beings. He alone bears the sin of the world and he alone bears it away. . . . The powers of sin and death that have such a hold on us—*and that are at the root of all trauma*—are finally nullified.[39]

It is as both the crucified and risen Lord that Jesus Christ bears away the sin of the world. In him, we have hope that death and sin have been overcome. He did not just suffer the misery of our sin and allow himself to become subject to our trauma. Nor did he descend into the lowest depths of hell just to join us there. Christ bears all these unbearable things *pro nobis*, so that he might bear them away. It is this overwhelming love that Jesus speaks of in the parable, a love that runs toward those who are lost in the far country, even if it means that he must descend to the depths of hell to meet them there. The church is called to embrace those who have suffered the soul wounds of combat trauma with the same reckless

39. Hunsinger, *Bearing the Unbearable*, 13–14.

abandon. When those who have suffered the souls wounds of war return to the community of faith from the far country, we need to restore them to the full life of faith with celebration.[40]

In *The Return of the Prodigal Son*, Henri Nouwen suggests that pastors might envision themselves as the father in the parable welcoming home God's other sons and daughters. This is the high honor that pastoral caregivers have, to receive combat veterans back into the life of faith and help to connect or reconnect them with the wider community of faith. Ultimately, that hope is met in an encounter with the Father.[41] To be welcomed and forgiven by the Father—as the prodigal son was welcomed and forgiven, as Christ himself was welcomed—is to return home. The journey home for survivors of trauma is to come to know that they are forgiven and were held in the embrace of God's love all along. The Father's love remained for them even while they were cut off in the far country.

Those welcomed home and reconciled to God through faith are simultaneously sent out as witnesses to the good news they have received. Barth explains the role of the pastoral caregiver thus:

> In the cure of souls, he accepts responsibility for his new or newly confirmed membership of the community of knowledge and witness. He does so by inviting him to be open, by listening in a spirit of openness, and by assisting him by pointing to the Word of God which nourishes him also to temporal and eternal life. It means helping another by making clear to him that *he is ordained a witness of Jesus Christ and that he is usable as such.*[42]

It is in the Word of God that war wounded souls find both their welcome home and the new found task to be sent out as Jesus's

---

40. We must always be wary of premature forgiveness or cheap grace. Forgiveness should never be used to deny or cover over the painful realities of war. See Brock and Lettini, *Soul Repair*, 102–103.

41. To this point, Nouwen thinks a more apt title for the parable would be "the parable of the Father's love." See Nouwen, *Prodigal Son*, 93.

42. Barth, *CD*, 4.3.2:886, emphasis added.

witnesses. By no means does this mean parading veterans as "tokens" in front of a church congregation (or any other audience), much less a soldier who, perhaps now, has difficulty with large crowds. Nor does it necessarily mean enlisting such survivors to our causes of war or peace.[43] Above and beyond any survivor mission, those who have been welcomed home from war by the Father have been called and will be equipped by the Spirit as witnesses of Jesus Christ.

## Conclusion

I have suggested that pastoral caregivers provide sanctuary and encourage lament and confession, all with an aim toward forgiveness and reconciliation for those who have suffered the soul wound of trauma. That is not to say this must be the outline of every single pastoral encounter with those who return home from war. It is simply to offer the riches of the Christian tradition that may be brought to bear in the care of soul wounds and to locate them along a trajectory toward reconciliation. The wounds of war are deep and many, if not most, live with them for a lifetime. Faith does not solve our problems, but reminds us that, in the midst of any problem, God alone is our help and comfort. In this vein, Thurneysen argues that this drives pastoral care toward an anthropology rooted in baptism. He writes: "For baptism is the sign that man in and with his whole double nature, his conscious and his unconscious, in short in his totality or, to quote once more from the Catechism, 'With body and soul, both in life and death, is not his own, but belongs to his faithful Savior Jesus Christ.'"[44] In body and soul, in life and death, we belong to Jesus Christ. On Holy Saturday, we find that our trauma, soul wounds, and god-forsakenness, too, are brought into the very heart of God in Christ. The death suffered, even in life, is borne by our faithful Savior. The remainders and

---

43. I do, however, think that the voices of soldiers and veterans are vital to ecclesial and national conversations about war and peace.

44. Thurneysen, *Pastoral Care*, 97.

fragments of life that remain on the other side of trauma, those, too, belong to Jesus Christ. In God's presence, through lament and confession, those painful and enigmatic pieces are brought to the Father as we are joyously received into his loving arms.

I began chapter 1 with this quote from Tyler Boudreau:

> They say war is hell, but I say it's the foyer to hell. I say coming home is hell and hell ain't got no coordinates. You can't find it on the charts because there are no charts. Hell is no place at all, so when you're there, you're nowhere—you're lost. The narrative, that's your chart, your own story. There are guys who come home from war and live fifty years without a narrative, fifty years lost. They don't even know their own story, never have, and never will. But they're moving amidst the text every day and every long night without even realizing it. . . . They live inside the narrative like a cell, and their only escape is to understand its dimensions.[45]

In the end, it is the narrative that is the key. Surely, this is what pastors and chaplains must excel at: listening to and telling stories, connecting soldiers' stories with the gospel story. Without that story, we are all lost. Narrative psychotherapies, like those described by Herman and others, can help survivors piece together their own story, but they do not connect them with the ultimately "therapeutic"—that is, salvific—story. Each aspect of ministering to soul wounds that I have described is about helping those who have suffered combat trauma connect their story to the story of the God who, in Christ, has descended into hell for us. We cannot properly understand our own story and our place in that narrative until we come to know the story of God's overwhelming love that has overcome our trauma and our sin through cross, grave, and resurrection. This is the hope "of those who weep / and of those who weep with those who weep."[46]

---

45. Boudreau, *Packing Inferno*, quoted in Brock and Lettini, *Soul Repair*, 65.

46. Weems, *Psalms of Lament*, xvii.

# 5

# Ministering Between Cross and Resurrection

HOLY SATURDAY IS THE space of death between cross and resurrection. It is marked by silence and absence. In chapter 4, I provided a suggestion for the form spiritual care might take for those who are stuck in the far country with soul wounds from combat trauma. The Holy Saturday experience of the hiddenness of God may be acute for those living in the wake of trauma and moral injury. For those in the far country, God's seeming silence may be deafening in the face of evil and death. What of those who minister to those who have survived the trials of combat and come home? What might it mean for them to minister from within this dark day itself? In Christ's descent into hell, he meets those who suffer the hell of war and the hell of coming home. On the cross and in the grave, God makes his company with those who suffer. In the bottomless abyss of sin and death, Christ has descended to the furthest depths of our sorrow.

Holy Saturday is not just the theological space into which pastoral caregivers might invite those who have survived trauma. I contend that it is the place pastoral caregivers must also make their home. Rather than simply point others toward an open door, pastors and chaplains may invite those who have suffered the spiritual wounds of war to enter into the room as guests. This sort of hospitality may only be extended if pastoral caregivers themselves have walked through the door and have been welcomed into the place where God's death and love meet on this day of deep mystery. The Apostle Paul invites the church into just this sort of ministry. He says:

> Do you not know that all of us who have been baptized into Christ Jesus were baptized into his death? Therefore, we have been buried with him by baptism into death, so that, just as Christ was raised from the dead by the glory of the Father, so we, too, might walk in newness of life. (Rom 6:3–4)

In baptism, we have joined Christ in the grave. The church, then, is Christ's buried body in the world.

To provide such a witness, pastoral caregivers must be on the journey of faith through prayer. Alan Lewis writes:

> For surely it is only in the mode of prayer—in meditation, reflection, and straining of the heart and ear for a word of God beyond human speechlessness, that one could finally do justice to a narrative like ours which, at its center point, has God buried in a grave on Easter Saturday. What is there left to do *but* pray, if the story of God's own death and burial be true?[1]

Ministers must recognize their fundamental weakness and dependence on God that has been revealed fully on Holy Saturday. As I examine what it means to minister from Holy Saturday, it will first be seen that pastoral care can only be given if it is through dependence on God in prayer. In, with, and through prayer, pastors and chaplains may invite those who come home from war into God's sacred presence. Next, in *The Wounded Healer*, Henri Nouwen provides a fitting image for the sort of minister that might beckon war wounded souls into *sanctuary, lament and confession*, and *forgiveness and reconciliation* as outlined in chapter 4. Ministers also stand before God wounded and are "called to not only to care for their own wounds and the wounds of others, but also to make their

---

1. Lewis, *Between Cross and Resurrection*, 463.

wounds into a major source of healing power."[2] I will examine what it means for pastoral caregivers to be "wounded healers." I will also close with some brief thoughts on what it means for those who come home from war to be on a spiritual journey from the hell of the far country to their true home with God.

## Holy Saturday and Prayer

After trauma, hope may be impossible to imagine. Prayer itself may seem an impossibility. Lewis wonders as much:

> What is the point of praying to the God of the cross whose power and wisdom are only those of impotence and foolishness?
>
> The answer, surely, as discomforting as it is hopeful, makes costly demands even as it liberates. For if the surrender of power is *the* form, and the only form, that God's power takes, and if vulnerable self-abandonment is itself the creative energy which is bringing history powerfully to its fulfillment, that places an unbearable demand upon ourselves who in and through words and deeds of prayerful living would align and associate ourselves with the triune history of God, confessing and obeying Christ's cruciform, grave-shaped lordship over all. Such prayer must humanly enact the divine possibility of grace—that those and only those who lose themselves shall find themselves. To pray to the crucified God is, therefore, to affirm and practice radical dependence and surrender to the point of death itself—which may be why so few of us know how to pray, or even wish to do so.[3]

The Holy Saturday witness of pastoral caregivers must begin in prayer. For it is through prayer that we come to know our utter dependence on God. On Holy Saturday, the vanity of our human

---

2. Nouwen, *Wounded Healer*, 88–89.

3. Lewis, *Between Cross and Resurrection*, 303.

efforts toward autonomy are laid to waste. On this day, history is revealed for what it is—hubris and failure. As Christ's buried body, sent out into the world, the church is sustained by prayerfully trusting in God alone. Pastoral caregivers must be sustained by such faith.

Barth suggests that God's command that we pray is proof that God has "made common cause with man and wills to do so again."[4] Indeed, prayer is a sign of God's solidarity with the cause of those who have experienced the horrible traumas of war. God in Christ intercedes for us before the heavenly throne of grace and, when we pray, we join Christ, already at prayer on our behalf. We pray not of our own power, but in the power of the Holy Spirit within us. It is the Spirit who carries our prayers to God and redeems them even though our words are often stuttered, mumbled, inadequate, imperfect, and touched by sin. Paul says that the "Spirit helps us in our weakness; for we do not know how to pray as we ought, but that the very Spirit intercedes with sighs too deep for words. And God, who searches the heart, knows what is the mind of the Spirit, because the Spirit intercedes for the saints according to the will of God" (Rom 8:26–27). Our prayer is to God, in God, and through God. As such, we may—indeed, must—relinquish all pretense and pride. Prayer, Barth says:

> Does not have to be beautiful or edifying, logically coherent or theologically correct. Neither formally, materially, nor methodically does it have to display any kind of art.... Where man is concerned only with God he knows that he needs no alien art but must capitulate with all his arts. The only thing that counts is that he should really be concerned with God and with a request addressed to him. It may well be that he can only sigh, stammer, and mutter.[5]

Christ's cross and grave demand our complete honesty before God. Perhaps as pastoral caregivers hear the stories of those who

---

4. Barth, *CD*, 3.4:88.
5. Barth, *CD*, 3.4:88.

weep after war, they too can only sigh, stammer, and mutter in the face of evil and death. These, too, are the prayers we bring to our heavenly Father.

In chapter 2, I examined Psalm 88 as a test case for the scriptural warrant for a theology of Holy Saturday. There I suggested that Psalm 88 should be read as Christ's own prayer from the grave. It was also seen that the church should join Christ in praying this prayer. Just as the church aligns itself in solidarity with the cause of Christ, pastoral caregivers, through prayer, may join in solidarity with the cause of those who have suffered horrific trauma. Pastoral caregivers pray even (and especially) when those who suffer cannot. I am reminded of the member of my home congregation I wrote of in chapter 1 who told me that she would be praying on my behalf until I could. It is this sort of solidarity and intercession that is demanded if pastoral caregivers are to witness to God's solidarity with us in Christ. In this solidarity, pastoral caregivers must surrender themselves completely to God's grace. Lewis writes:

> Yet is not all prayer designed for Easter Saturday, the product of confusion, emptiness, and grief? Prayer is desperation translated into daring—the risk of letting go of confidence, eloquence, and that "spirituality," so fashionable now but so seductive. To pray is to confess not the abundance but the exhaustion of one's verbal, intellectual, and spiritual resources. It is surrender to one who prays for us when we have no prayers left and can only do so only when we acknowledge our own bankruptcy of spirit.[6]

Ministers must acknowledge the bankruptcy of their own spirits and pray in the power of God's Holy Spirit alone. It is through the humility and brokenness of the pastoral caregiver that an honest witness may be given to Christ's cross and grave.

---

6. Lewis, *Between Cross and Resurrection*, 464.

"What is there left to do *but* pray, if the story of God's own death and burial be true?"[7] Lewis reminds us that, as witnesses to this great mystery, pastoral care must begin and end in prayer:

> Prayer then, the sound of silence upon Easter Saturday and every day which reenacts it, is the last breath of our self-relinquishment, the freedom we give God at last to *be* God, gracious, holy, and creative, precisely in those cries where our bodies, intellects, and souls cry out in tears of anger and bewilderment that God is dead.[8]

Pastoral caregivers witness to this Word of God, divested of their own power, their own faith in their method, education, or personality, and cast their lot fully with the God who has made his place with us in the grave. It is only when pastoral caregivers themselves stand before God's presence in prayer that they may invite those for whom they care into that same presence. It is this presence that provides true *sanctuary*. It is this presence to whom all *lament and confession* must ultimately be addressed. It is from this presence that the word of *forgiveness and reconciliation* may be heard. Thus, all pastoral care with those who suffer trauma must proceed from prayer and lead those with soul wounds to it. It is in prayer that we expose our wounded selves before the only one who can heal them. It is through prayer that pastoral caregivers invite those for whom they care into the theological space of Holy Saturday.

## The Pastoral Caregiver as Wounded Healer

I have suggested that combat trauma may be understood as a wound that touches not only body and mind but also soul. This soul wound leaves combat veterans stuck in the far country, seemingly abandoned by God. In combat and after coming home, soldiers may wonder if they indeed have been left to suffer the symptoms of PTSD and the painful questions that refuse easy answers alone. I have also suggested that this experience of God's hiddenness is an

---

7. Lewis, *Between Cross and Resurrection*, 463.
8. Lewis, *Between Cross and Resurrection*, 464.

echo of Christ's own abandonment by God in death on Holy Saturday. Christ joins those who have suffered trauma, indeed joins in solidarity with all humanity, by taking on sin and death and drinking fully from the cup of God's wrath. It is through this act of love within the triune life of God that our sins are finally borne away. Because Christ has descended into the hell of our every brokenness, we may now find that it is precisely in our wounds that Christ chooses to be God with us. The ministry of pastoral caregivers should embody this witness. Caregivers stand with those for whom they care as deeply wounded persons. Neither pastors nor anyone else but Christ alone can bear our sins away and save us. Nevertheless, Henri Nouwen argues that our own wounds may point others toward the healing found in Christ.[9]

For Nouwen, loneliness best describes the condition of human brokenness—that alienation and separation from one another and God that we experience as a result of sin. The experience of loneliness is certainly a fitting description of those on the other side of trauma. Trauma, by its very nature, is an isolating event. It creates a rupture and break in human life and community. In war, it separates soldiers from their enemy, from their fellow soldiers, and from themselves. Time itself seems ruptured as the past trauma continues to be re-experienced as a vivid, present reality. No one else experiences these particular dark thoughts and nightmares. The one who suffers trauma suffers alone. As previously argued, those who suffer trauma may even perceive that God himself has left them alone in the midst of the traumas of war. Those caught in this acute experience of loneliness may seek experiences of connection in unhealthy and even dangerous ways. The personal euphoria found walking the line between life and death in combat may be sought through any number of high-risk behaviors when soldiers return home. Connection may be found in unhealthy relationships and meaningless sexual encounters. Nouwen finds such immediate relief and satisfaction to be false gods. He writes:

---

9. See Nouwen, *Wounded Healer*.

> When we are impatient, when we want to give up our loneliness and try to overcome the separation and incompleteness we feel, we easily relate to our human world with devastating expectations. We ignore what we already know with a deep-seated intuitive knowledge—that no love or friendship, no intimate embrace or tender kiss, no community, commune, or collective, no man or woman, will ever be able to satisfy our desire to be released from our lonely condition.[10]

These false hopes can only lead to bitterness when such expectations remain unrealized.

Nouwen thinks that the deep wound of our loneliness may actually be a source of understanding and healing. He writes: "The wound of loneliness is actually like the Grand Canyon—a deep incision in the surface of our existence that has become an inexhaustible source of beauty and self-understanding. . . . The Christian way of life does not take away our loneliness; it protects and cherishes it as a precious gift."[11] Can it be otherwise? At the center of the confession of the Christian faith lies the claim that God himself descended into death and hell. In Jesus, God lives this loneliness unto death on a cross and abandonment of God by God. Faith does not overcome our loneliness, it means we courageously live within it.

It is no surprise, then, that Nouwen finds loneliness at the center of the personal and professional experience of ministers. For him, this experience is not something to be overcome, rather, it is to be acknowledged and put at the service of the healing of others. Nouwen is not suggesting a "spiritual exhibitionism." He writes: "Ministers who talk in the pulpit about their own personal problems are of no help to their congregation, for suffering people are not helped by those who tell them that they have the same problems."[12] Pastors and chaplains need not have experienced

---

10. Nouwen, *Wounded Healer*, 90–91.

11. Nouwen, *Wounded Healer*, 90.

12. Nouwen, *Wounded Healer*, 94. Bonhoeffer makes a similar suggestion: "It would certainly be most misleading to remove the distance between pastor

combat trauma to minister to those who have. Rather, "Making one's own wounds a source of healing" calls for "a constant willingness to see one's own pain and suffering as rising from the depth of the human condition we all share."[13] Pastoral caregivers share the common lot of sin, death, and loneliness with all for whom they care, including those who bear the wounds of war. For Nouwen, this sort of ministry is an embodiment of hospitality.

At the outset of this chapter, I hinted at this ministry of hospitality that pastoral caregivers might provide. Those who minister to those living in the far country after war can invite those who suffer to find healing in the theological space of Holy Saturday only by ministering from within that space themselves. Not as one who has necessarily been traumatized, but as one who has heard God's Word for him on that day, too. This begins with compassionate prayer—prayer that is only possible from a place of deep honesty about one's own wounds. If pastors deign to invite others to meet Christ in the depths of their pain, ministers must themselves live in the presence of the risen Christ who has made his home in the grave. It is from this place that pastoral caregivers may be hosts that "feel at home in their own house" and "create a free and fearless place for the unexpected visitor."[14]

Henri Nouwen thinks that to provide such a welcome requires "the ability to pay attention to the guest."[15] This is an "attention

---

and parishioner which is established by God's commission. The pastor should not—out of a misguided idea of solidarity—speak about personal unworthiness or sin. As a rule, this is not helpful for the other person. By doing this, we interpose ourselves and our own problems between the other person and Christ. It could also be an evasion of the mission of spiritual care. The relationship may proceed naturally to the point where one doesn't know who is the pastor and who is parishioner. But we shouldn't make a method of that which is an ultimate possibility and a genuine grace. The office of spiritual care does not exist to declare solidarity but to listen and to proclaim the gospel. Proper distance helps establish proper closeness" (Bonhoeffer, *Spiritual Care*, 37).

13. Nouwen, *Wounded Healer*, 94–95.
14. Nouwen, *Wounded Healer*, 96.
15. Nouwen, *Wounded Healer*, 96.

without intention."¹⁶ It is the ability to be present, sympathetic, and open to the needs of guests. The minister should allow wounded souls to come on their own terms, without seeking to inappropriately fulfill needs through them. This is what Nouwen means by feeling at home in our own house. This attention without intention is one necessary precondition in order for pastoral caregivers to provide *sanctuary* to those who have suffered trauma. This sort of concentration is won, Nouwen says, "paradoxically, by withdrawing into ourselves, not out of self-pity but out of humility." In doing so, "we create the space for others to be themselves and to come to us on their own terms."¹⁷ This withdrawal is to find Christ's presence at the very center of our brokenness. If pastoral caregivers minister from this center, they "can be free to let others enter into the space created for them, and allow them to dance their own dance, sing their own song, and speak their own language without fear." Such a pastoral presence is "no longer threatening and demanding, but inviting and liberating."¹⁸

Pastoral caregivers may only welcome those who have suffered trauma as guests into the theological space of Holy Saturday if they have already made it a comfortable home. From this home, caregivers may offer much needed space for the wounded soul who returned from war to find Christ's own descent into hell at the very center of their spiritual pain rather than seeking its abatement in ways that are doomed to perpetual frustration. Nouwen suggests that such hospitality provides the opportunity for understanding and freedom:

> Many people in this life suffer because they are anxiously searching for the man or woman, the event or encounter, which will take their loneliness away. But when they enter a house with real hospitality, they soon see that their own wounds must be understood, not as sources of despair

---

16. Nouwen, *Wounded Healer*, 97.
17. Nouwen, *Wounded Healer*, 97.
18. Nouwen, *Wounded Healer*, 98.

and bitterness, but as signs that they have to travel on in obedience to the calling sounds of those wounds.[19]

The calling sounds of the soul wounds of war invite those who have suffered trauma to enter into *lament and confession* and find *forgiveness and reconciliation* precisely in the place of their greatest fear and deepest pain.[20] To wonder at God's presence and love is to draw near to the deepest mystery of God on Holy Saturday.

There is no route around such pain or easy balm for such wounds of the soul. Pastoral caregivers are not interested in helping people escape from suffering, but rather in helping them enter into it rightly. This sort of welcome can only be made by one who is not running away from her own suffering. Nouwen writes:

> Ministers are not doctors whose primary task is to take away pain. Rather, they deepen the pain to a level where it can be shared. When people come with their loneliness to ministers, they can expect that their loneliness will be understood and felt, so that they no longer have to run away from it, but can accept it as an expression of the basic human condition.[21]

---

19. Nouwen, *Wounded Healer*, 98–99.

20. In chapter 4, I hinted that *sanctuary, lament and confession*, and *forgiveness and reconciliation* were not neat, linear stages through which one progresses and leaves behind all previous concerns and cares. Thus, pastoral caregivers need not worry about checklists, progressions, or stages of spiritual growth. Their concern must be to welcome their guest into the theological space of Holy Saturday as they are. Pastoral caregivers, freed from the anxiety of running away from their own suffering, are open to meet war wounded souls in just such a way.

21. Nouwen, *Wounded Healer*, 99. Put another way, Hunsinger writes: "Severe emotional pain cannot be endured if it does not have a relational home, someone to hold what cannot be borne. Ministers of the gospel of Jesus Christ who are rooted and grounded in the love of God provide just such a relational home for all those who groan for the redemption of the world. They offer a steady, sturdy, compassionate, and loving witness to all who have suffered trauma. In so far as they thus participate in Christ's own compassion, they become witnesses to and mediators of Christ's miraculous grace" (Hunsinger, *Bearing the Unbearable*, 18). I think Hunsinger points to both Nouwen's concern that wounded healers create a hospitable space for wounded others, as well as my suggestion that Holy Saturday is, in fact, this sort of space within the life of

## Ministering Between Cross and Resurrection

God in Christ has joined in solidarity with the cause of humanity. On Holy Saturday, our pain and suffering have become God's. Our loneliness has become God's. All sin and evil have been borne by God and borne away. From Holy Saturday, pastoral caregivers may invite those who have suffered deep trauma to find that, in the grave, Christ beckons us to follow him and to be "united with him in a death like his" (Rom 6:5). This alone is the path to life. We need no longer run from our loneliness or sense of God-abandonment; rather, we are invited to find that in our wounds—even in the depths of hell—Christ has made his home with us.

## In the End: A Holy Saturday Pilgrimage

Pastoral caregivers should not only be grounded in a theology of Holy Saturday but they must also take up spiritual residence there. Pastoral caregivers may only invite others into Holy Saturday as they have made it a home for themselves. This begins in prayerful solidarity with those who suffer the spiritual wounds of war. It also demands that pastoral caregivers become at home within themselves that they might be gracious hosts to those for whom they care. Pastors and chaplains should be "wounded healers" who are able to provide meaningful hospitality to those who return from war. They are called to provide hospitality that gives full attention to the needs of the other and space for the other to enter into her own suffering rather than seeking to overcome it in superficial ways. On Holy Saturday, those who come home from war are invited to find that Christ is present in the hell of war and in the hell of coming home.

I firmly believe that this world is a Holy Saturday world, mired as it is in sin and death. Perhaps then, the entirety of the Christian life in this world may be seen as a pilgrim journey between cross and resurrection. For each one of us, life is a far country journey as we strive to make our way to our true home. To take up one's cross and to follow Christ is a journey of self-denial

---

God and the theological room ministers might also occupy.

and self-renunciation before God—in short, the very death of the self.[22] This journey of sanctification is lifelong, as we await the revelation of our true selves that yet lie hidden with Christ. As Paul says: "For you have died, and your life is hidden with Christ in God. When Christ who is your life is revealed, then you also will be revealed with him in glory" (Col 3:3–4).

Until that revelation, we are called to be a people of prayer. This prayer is not of our own power or for our own ends. As Lewis points out:

> Those who intercede for the needs of others, or pray for deliverance from evil, iconoclastically admit that collectively the human race, supposedly so successful and mature, is unable to liberate itself, heal its own diseases, comfort its own fears, solve its own problems or control its own destiny. And if, in the midst of inadequacy, suffering, malevolence, and death, in despair for ourselves or for our world, Christian prayer peters out into speechlessness and mumbling, leaving God's own Spirit to sigh ineffably on our behalf, that very silence, human and divine, rebukes the wordy noisomeness and empty rhetoric of our self-promoting age.[23]

Indeed, this is where the psalmist leaves us at the end of Psalm 88, in silence. This, too, is how pastors and chaplains must often meet those who suffer. We have now returned to Walter Brueggemann's point that faith does not give us the answers to all of life's questions. Pastoral caregivers do not meet the traumatized with answers. The chaos and ambiguity of life remain, even for the faithful. From Holy Saturday, we can see that the resurrection provides no justification for us to hope in any particular this-worldly outcomes. PTSD symptoms may persist and the struggle to come home from war may be lifelong. On Holy Saturday, we are reminded that each one of us will also go to the grave. There is no easy jump in the gospel narrative from cross to resurrection—there is a radical break.

---

22. For Calvin, this self-denial is the sum of the Christian life. See Calvin, *Institutes*, 1:689–712.

23. Lewis, *Between Cross and Resurrection*, 307.

To remember that Christ's horrific passion and joyous resurrection are absolutely discontinuous events is to bear witness to this break that is Holy Saturday. In this discontinuity, we are reminded that our daily call of discipleship is to die with Christ. As those who weep with those who weep, we also hold fast to our sure hope that we will one day rise with him. This is the path through hell that Christ has walked ahead of us. The path that we, too, are called to follow.

# Bibliography

Ackerman, Spencer. "25 Tons of Bombs Wipe Afghan Town Off Map." *Wired*, 19 January 2011. https://www.wired.com/2011/01/25-tons-of-bombs-wipes-afghan-town-off-the-map.

———. "Why I Flattened Three Afghan Villages." *Wired*, 1 February 2011. https://www.wired.com/2011/02/i-flattened-afghan-villages.

Alighieri, Dante. *The Divine Comedy: Inferno*. Translated by Mark Musa. New York: Penguin, 1971.

American Psychiatric Association. *Diagnostic and Statistical Manual of Mental Disorders: DSM-V*. Washington, DC: American Psychiatric Association, 2013.

Balthasar, Hans Urs von. *Heart of the World*. Translated by Erasmo S. Leiva. San Francisco: Ignatius, 1989.

———. *Mysterium Paschale*. Translated by Aidan Nichols. San Francisco: Ignatius, 1990.

———. "We Walked Where There Was No Path." In *You Crown the Year with your Goodness: Sermons Through the Liturgical Year*, 87–92. Translated by Graham Harrison. San Francisco: Ignatius, 1989.

Barth, Karl. *Church Dogmatics*. Edited by G. W. Bromiley and T. F. Torrance. Translated by G. T. Thomson and Harold Knight. 14 vols. New York: T & T Clark, 2004.

———. *Credo*. New York: Scribner, 1962.

———. *The Faith of the Church: A Commentary on the Apostles' Creed According to Calvin's Catechism*, edited by Jean-Louis Leuba. Translated by Gabriel Vahanian. New York: Meridian, 1958.

Bermejo, Bartolome. *Christ Leading the Patriarchs to Paradise*. 1480, tempera on wood, Institute of Hispanic Art, Barcelona.

Bonhoeffer, Dietrich. *Life Together and Prayerbook of the Bible*. Vol. 5 of *Dietrich Bonhoeffer Works*. Edited by Geifrey B. Kelly. Translated by Daniel W. Bloesch and James H. Burtness. Minneapolis: Fortress, 2005.

———. *Spiritual Care*. Translated by Jay C. Rochelle. Philadelphia: Fortress, 1985.

Broadwell, Paula, and Vernon Loeb. *All In: The Education of General David Petraeus*. New York: Penguin, 2012.

# Bibliography

Brock, Rita Nakashima, and Gabriella Lettini. *Soul Repair: Recovering from Moral Injury After War*. Boston: Beacon, 2012.

Brueggemann, Walter. *Abiding Astonishment: Psalms, Modernity, and the Making of History*. Louisville: Westminster John Knox, 1991.

———. Foreword to *Psalms of Lament*, by Ann Weems, ix–xii. Louisville: Westminster John Knox, 1995.

———. *The Message of the Psalm: a Theological Commentary*. Minneapolis: Fortress, 1984.

———. *Praying the Psalms*. Winona, MN: Saint Mary's, 1993.

Calhoun, Lawrence, and Richard Tedeschi. *Facilitating Posttraumatic Growth: A Clinician's Guide*. Mahwah, NJ: Lawrence Erlbaum Associates, 1999.

Calvin, John. *Institutes of the Christian Religion*. Vol. 1. Edited by John T. McNeil. Translated by Ford Lewis Battles. Louisville: Westminster John Knox, 1960.

Campbell, Keith. "NT Lament in Current Research and its Implications for American Evangelicals." *Journal of the Evangelical Theological Society* 57 (2014) 757–60.

Carlson, Eve B., et al. "Traumatic Stressor Exposure and Post-Traumatic Symptoms in Homeless Veterans." *Military Medicine* 178 (2013) 970–73.

Connell, Martin F. "Descensus Christi Ad Infernos: Christ's Descent to the Dead." *Theological Studies* 62 (2001) 262–82.

Dionysius and his workshop (Moscow School). *Descent into Hell*. 1495-1504, tempera on wood, State Russian Museum, Saint Petersburg.

Dykstra, Robert C. "Rending the Curtain: Lament as an Act of Vulnerable Aggression." In *Lament: Reclaiming Practices in Pulpit, Pew, and Public Square*, edited by Sally A. Brown and Patrick D. Miller, 59–69. Louisville: Westminster John Knox, 2005.

Engdahl, B., et al. "Post-Traumatic Stress Disorder: a Right Temporal Lobe Syndrome?" *Journal of Neural Engineering* 7 (2010) 1–8.

Grudem, Wayne. "He Did Not Descend into Hell: A Plea for Following Scripture Instead of the Apostle's Creed." *Journal of the Evangelical Theological Society* 34 (1991) 103–13.

———. *Systematic Theology*. Grand Rapids: Zondervan, 1994.

Hauerwas, Stanley. *War and the American Difference: Theological Reflections on Violence and National Identity*. Grand Rapids: Baker Academic, 2011.

Herman, Judith. *Trauma and Recovery: The Aftermath of Violence—from Domestic Abuse to Political Terror*. New York: Basic, 1997.

Hunsinger, Deborah van Deusen. *Bearing the Unbearable: Trauma, Gospel, and Pastoral Care*. Grand Rapids: Eerdmans, 2015.

———. *Theology and Pastoral Counseling: A New Interdisciplinary Approach*. Grand Rapids: Eerdmans, 1995.

Hunsinger, George. *How to Read Karl Barth: The Shape of His Theology*. New York: Oxford University Press, 1991.

———. "The Sinner and the Victim." In *The T&T Clark Companion to the Doctrine of Sin*, edited by Keith Johnson and David Lauber, 433-449. New York: Bloomsbury T&T Clark, 2016.
Jordan, William Chester. "A Fresh Look at Medieval Sanctuary." In *Law and the Illicit in Medieval Europe*, edited by Ruth Mazo Karras et al., 17-32. Philadelphia: University of Pennsylvania Press, 2008.
Jungel, Eberhart. *God as the Mystery of the World: On the Foundation of the Theology of the Crucified One in the Dispute Between Theism and Atheism*. Translated by Darrell Guder. Grand Rapids: Eerdmans, 1983.
Kinghorn, Warren. "Combat Trauma and Moral Fragmentation: A Theological Account of Moral Injury." *Journal of the Society of Christian Ethics* 2 (2012) 57-74.
Kolb, Robert, and Timothy J. Wengert, eds. *The Book of Concord: The Confessions of the Evangelical Lutheran Church*. Translated by Charles Arand et al. Minneapolis: Fortress, 2000.
Lauber, David. *Barth on the Descent into Hell: God, Atonement and the Christian Life*. Burlington, VT: Ashgate, 2004.
———. "Hell" In *The Westminster Handbook to Karl Barth*, edited by Richard Burnett, 93-94. Louisville: Westminster John Knox, 2013.
Lewis, Alan. *Between Cross and Resurrection: A Theology of Holy Saturday*. Grand Rapids: Eerdmans, 2001.
Litz, Brett T., et al. "Moral Injury and Moral Repair in War Veterans: A Preliminary Model and Intervention." *Clinical Psychology Review* 29 (2009) 695-706.
———. *Adaptive Disclosure: A New Treatment for Military Loss, Trauma, and Moral Injury*. New York: Guilford, 2016.
Luther, Martin. *The Complete Sermons of Martin Luther*. Vol. 5. Edited by Eugene F. A. Klug. Translated by Eugene F. A. Klug et al. Grand Rapids: Baker, 2000.
Maguen, Shira, and Brett Litz. "Moral Injury in Veterans of War." *PTSD Research Quarterly* 23 (2012) 1-3.
Mockenhaupt, Brian. "The Last Patrol." *The Atlantic*, November 2010. https://www.theatlantic.com/magazine/archive/2010/11/the-last-patrol/308266.
Nouwen, Henri. *The Return of the Prodigal Son: A Story of Homecoming*. New York: Doubleday, 1994.
———. *The Wounded Healer: Ministry in Contemporary Society*. New York: Image Doubleday, 2010.
Pelikan, Jaroslav, and Valerie Hotchkiss, eds. *Creeds and Confessions of Faith in the Christian Tradition*. 4 vols. New Haven: Yale University Press, 2003.
Pitstick, Alyssa. *Light in Darkness: Hans Urs von Balthasar and the Catholic Doctrine of Christ's Descent into Hell*. Grand Rapids: Eerdmans, 2007.
Rahner, Karl. *The Trinity*. New York: Continuum, 2001.
Rambo, Shelly. *Spirit and Trauma: A Theology of Remaining*. Louisville: Westminster John Knox, 2010.

Rist, Johann von. "O Darkest Woe, 332." In *Evangelical Lutheran Hymnary*, edited by Evangelical Lutheran Synod. St. Louis: MorningStar Music, 1996.

Schaff, Philip, and Henry Wace, eds. *Nicene and Post-Nicene Fathers of the Christian Church*. Vol. 7. New York: Christian Literature, 1894.

Shay, Jonathan. *Achilles in Vietnam: Combat Trauma and Undoing of Character*. New York: Scribner, 1994.

———. *Odysseus in America: Combat Trauma and the Trials of Homecoming*. New York: Scribner, 2002.

Taylor, Rob. "Death Comes from Far Away in Afghan Valley." *Reuters*, 19 July 2010. https://www.reuters.com/article/us-afghanistan-outpost-sniper/death-comes-from-far-away-in-afghan-valley-idUSTRE66J08I20100720.

Teresa, Mother, and Brian Kolodiejchuk. *Come Be My Light: The Private Writings of the Saint of Calcutta*. New York: Doubleday Religion, 2007.

Thurneysen, Eduard. *A Theology of Pastoral Care*. Translated by Jack A. Worthington and Thomas Wieser. Eugene, OR: Wipf and Stock, 2010.

Tietje, Adam. "Contra Rambo's 'Theology of Remaining': A Chalcedonian and Pastoral Conception of Trauma." *Pro Ecclesia* 28.1 (2019).

———. 2010–2011. "Faith and Doubt in the Arghandab." Unpublished manuscript.

———. "Home From the War." Memorial Service for Sergeant Justin Junkin, 3 October 2011, Memorial Chapel, Fort Campbell, KY. Homily.

———. "The Responsibility and Limits of Military Chaplains as Public Theologians." In Religious Studies Scholars as Public Intellectuals, edited by Sabrina D. MisirHiralall, Christopher L. Fici, and Gerald S. Vigna, 91-108. New York: Routledge, 2018.

Tillich, Paul. *Systematic Theology*. Vol. 1. Chicago: University of Chicago Press, 1973.

United States Army. "Health Promotion, Risk Reduction, Suicide Prevention: Report 2010." http://www.armyg1.army.mil/hr/suicide/docs/Commanders%20Tool%20Kit/HPRRSP_Report_2010_v00.pdf.

Weems, Ann. *Psalms of Lament*. Louisville: Westminster John Knox, 1995.

Worthington, Everett, and Diane Langberg. "Religious Considerations and Self-Forgiveness in Treating Complex Trauma and Moral Injury in Present and Former Soldiers." *Journal of Psychology and Theology* 40 (2012) 274–88.

www.ingramcontent.com/pod-product-compliance
Lightning Source LLC
Chambersburg PA
CBHW050834160426
43192CB00010B/2025